SCHOOL
Discipline

SCHOOL Discipline

Best Practices for Administrators

Second Edition

LOUIS ROSEN

CORWIN PRESS
A Sage Publications Company
Thousand Oaks, California

For information:

Corwin Press
A Sage Publications Company
2455 Teller Road
Thousand Oaks, California 91320
www.corwinpress.com

Sage Publications Ltd.
1 Oliver's Yard
55 City Road
London EC1Y 1SP
United Kingdom

Sage Publications India Pvt. Ltd.
B-42, Panchsheel Enclave
Post Box 4109
New Delhi 110 017 India

Printed in the United States of America.

Library of Congress Cataloging-in-Publication Data

Rosen, Louis, Ph.D.
School discipline: Best practices for administrators / Louis Rosen.—2nd ed.
    p. cm.
Includes bibliographical references and index.
ISBN 1-4129-1348-9 (cloth) — ISBN 1-4129-1349-7 (pbk.)
    1. School discipline—United States. 2. School administrators—
United States. I. Title.
LB3012.2.R67 2005
371.5—dc22

                                                      2004024590

This book is printed on acid-free paper.

05 06 07 08 09 10 9 8 7 6 5 4 3 2 1

Acquisitions Editor:	Elizabeth Brenkus
Editorial Assistant:	Candice L. Ling
Production Editor:	Laureen A. Shea
Copy Editor:	Terese Platten, Freelance Editorial Services
Typesetter:	C&M Digitals (P) Ltd.
Proofreader:	Kevin Gleason
Indexer:	Naomi Linzer
Cover Designer:	Michael Dubowe
Graphic Designer:	Lisa Miller

Contents

List of Forms
and Figures

Preface

No school administrators in their right mind would ignore school discipline as one of their most important responsibilities. Nearly every survey of school administrators in recent years lists school discipline and school safety as one of or their most important areas of emphasis. Although serious acts of crime and violence are relatively rare in schools, fighting, bullying, acts of disrespect, and insubordination still remain as problems faced by school administrators every day. A study by Public Agenda (Johnson, 2004) indicated that seven in ten middle and high school teachers surveyed say their schools have serious problems with students who disrupt classes. Most experienced school administrators in charge of school discipline would say that students who continually disrupt classes make up less than 5% of students enrolled, but that 5% of enrolled students can take 90% of their time. What help exists for administrators involved with enforcing school discipline practices in schools? Unfortunately, not enough, considering the importance of the responsibility.

There is nothing that can erode the reputation of a school faster than poor school discipline. Unfortunately, one expulsion of a student having a gun on campus or a single sale of marijuana can override national merit scholarship winners and a state championship in football. Schools can become infamous for a single act of disruption. Most schools are known for their firm, fair, and consistent discipline practices. Unfortunately, the few schools with a dramatic instance of violence can taint all schools. Public relations has become an increasingly important area for school administrators.

There needs to be a special effort made to ensure that school discipline is not a vulnerable area for the reputation of a school or a school district. You cannot overstate the importance of good school discipline to public relations and the image the public has of schools. Too often school discipline is left to an overburdened assistant principal who is also responsible for school safety, attendance supervision, supervision of athletic events, and some portion of teacher evaluation. It is not possible for a single individual to deal with all the complex issues related to school discipline. School discipline practices must be a team effort and need to involve principals, counselors, teachers, superintendents, and school board members. School discipline policies need to be revised annually by a committee made up of the assistant principal in charge of discipline, at least two teachers, three students, two parents, two counselors, two members of the community, one school board member, one police officer, and one representative from the district office. The review needs to be done during the summer when representatives are free of distractions. The committee needs a generous budget that will help staff and provide proper plant requirements to ensure school safety and discipline.

Every effort must be made to ensure that school administrators are keeping up with research on what school safety and school discipline practices are being used, and which are most effective. The individual responsible for school discipline needs to have an up-to-date library on state and federal laws pertaining to suspension and expulsion. School disciplinarians need to be familiar with how the laws have been applied in their school district and their school. They must also be familiar with community factors which may impinge on the safety of their school. There also needs to be a working relationship between law enforcement and school building administrators. The assistant principal in charge of discipline needs to become an expert on school discipline practices and to pass that expertise on to the school discipline committee.

Research indicates that more teachers leave teaching because of discipline problems than any other reasons. Losing good teachers is a serious problem for all schools, be they public or private. A troublesome student can cause many a good teacher a loss of sleep and aggravation. Teachers enter the teaching field because they are interested in teaching not wrestling with students who continually disrupt classroom time. School administrators need to be a supportive tool of teachers in their classroom management routines and practices. Helping teachers have good classroom management practices has become an important part of the school disciplinarian's role.

Parental lack of control of their children and a failure to teach discipline at home may be chief reasons why students misbehave at school. The reality is that it is almost impossible for school administrators to influence what is happening at home. It is a difficult task, but school administrators must create such a strong environment at school that students are forced to adjust to the structured atmosphere of the school. This is no easy task. School administrators need all the help they can get. It needs to be a unified effort on the part of teachers, coaches, band directors, counselors, and all members of the school staff.

This book is primarily the result of a series of School Justice Institutes held in Los Angeles by the Center for Civic Education and training programs held in Washington, D.C., by the National Association of Secondary School Principals. The Institutes were titled *Principles and Practices of Justice on School Campuses*. Special programs were also conducted in Denver, Colorado; Sonoma, California; Providence, Rhode Island; Bowling Green, Ohio; and Orlando, Florida. These programs and Institutes invited assistant principals in charge of discipline to come together and share their problems and accomplishments related to school discipline practices. The programs and institutes provided these chosen school administrators with an opportunity to share their student codes of conduct and other forms and written materials. This text provides examples of the results of those institutes including opinions expressed.

The second edition has included much more research related to school discipline and school safety. The federal government has done some very excellent work in the field of school discipline and safety. Specific references and recommendations of those studies are contained in this newest edition. In Chapter 1, the goals of school discipline and definitions, as well as a checklist of fair discipline practices, remain intact, as does Chapter 2, standards of rule evaluation and model Student Codes of Conduct. Chapter 2 provides a compilation of the best of more than 50 codes of conduct from all over the nation. Chapter 3 provides suggestions and legal requirements related to consequences when students break school rules and district policies. Updates include timely issues such as the fairness of zero tolerance policies. Chapter 4 contains updated issues and laws related to suspension and expulsion. Chapter 5 has retained the classic court decisions that pertain to school discipline and includes several more recent rulings. Chapter 6 emphasizes research by the United States Department of Education and the Disciplined and Drug Free Schools Program. Chapter 7 is entirely new and describes prevention strategies including school climate, anger control, counseling, communication, documentation, and community involvement. Chapter 8 has been added due to the need for information related to disciplining special education students under the Individual Disabilities Education Act.

This book is not intended to be a complete resource text on school laws related to discipline. This would take a text by itself. It does try to be a summary of issues that school administrators need to address in order to keep from being unprepared for issues that may have serious consequences for the reputation and operation of their school. There are undoubtedly issues left out that may be important to some schools. It may be that a new book that emphasizes issues such as race and elementary education needs to be written, but this book focuses on secondary school discipline in mixed school populations. Superintendents and school board members may find that this book may help them understand the complexity of school discipline practices in the modern school. Professors of education hopefully will include school discipline as an important part of their school administration curriculum and may find this book an easy reference book for their students.

This text makes no attempt at criticism of contemporary practices of school discipline. It attempts only to describe what the common practices are and to describe practices that have been successful in recent years. The author supervised several programs for the Center for Civic Education as a grant administrator that took him to 18 states of the union. Included in those visitations were schools in inner cities, rural, and suburban areas. As a result of visiting hundreds of schools in various parts of the United States, the author believes that schools are for the most part well disciplined places where teachers can teach, and students can learn. There are districts, however, where financial difficulty or community problems have created an atmosphere of poor morale among teachers and administrators and that has influenced school discipline practices. Frequent turnover among administrators is also a problem in some school districts. Threats of being sued or taken to court, as well as legal preparation, have discouraged some of our best school administrators from staying in the field. Despite the handicaps, most school administrators have excellent judgment and are well equipped to deal with the problems they are confronted with each school year and each school day. School administrators are to be praised for the wonderful job they do. We hope that this text provides them with a few new ideas and reinforces the practices they already have in place. We also hope that school administrators new to their jobs will find this book helpful.

Acknowledgments

Corwin Press gratefully acknowledges the contributions of the following individuals:

Royce Avery
Principal
Dunbar Junior High School
Lubbock, TX

John Davis
Principal
Cabrillo Elementary School
Malibu, CA

J'Anne Ellsworth
Associate Professor
College of Education
Northern Arizona University
Flagstaff, AZ

Kay Insley
Assistant Principal
Highland Park Senior High School
Saint Paul, MN

Frank Kawtoski
Former Principal and Director of
    Secondary Education
Morrisville School District
Morrisville, PA

Gale Morrison
Professor
Graduate School of Education
University of California
Santa Barbara, CA

Janice Zuege
Associate Principal
Hortonville Middle School
Hortonville, WI

About the Author

Louis Rosen, PhD, is the executive director of the School Justice Institute, a nonprofit corporation dedicated to the improvement of fair discipline practices in schools. He has been a high school principal in the Los Angeles area for 19 years; an assistant principal for 4 years; a high school counselor; and a high school social studies teacher. He was the project director of the Drugs in the Schools and Principles and Practices of Justice on School Campuses programs for the Center for Civic Education in Calabasas, California. He has also served as the executive director of Partners of Education of Toledo for three years. While he was director of Partners in Education of Toledo, the organization provided more than 2,000 tutors and $2 million in resources for the public and Catholic schools of the Toledo area through partnerships with businesses and labor unions.

He is the author of *School Discipline Practices* and several journal articles that have appeared in the *The High School Journal*, a publication of the National Association of Secondary Schools Principals, and *School Safety*, published by the National School Safety Center. He was the principal writer of two student texts, *Drugs in the Schools* and *Violence in the Schools*, published by the Center for Civic Education. He has served as an academic specialist for the United States Information Agency and initiated a special program on school justice issues for Arab and Jewish principals in Israel.

He has a bachelor's degree in history from UCLA, a master's degree in secondary school administration from California State University at Los Angeles, and a PhD in education from Claremont Graduate University. He resides in Pacific Palisades, California. He currently serves as a volunteer for the Los Angeles Superior Court as a Court Appointed Special Advocate for Children (CASA). He also volunteers for Planned Parenthood of Los Angeles and serves on the board of the Southern California Regional Council of Organizations as their representative. He is currently working on a book: *College Is Not for Everyone*.

Fair Schoolwide Discipline

The word *discipline* is a strong word for most of us. It carries with it some preconceived descriptive words such as "weak," "strong," "good," and "bad." It is a word that has serious ramifications for all those who are engaged in the field of education. Having "good" discipline is a goal of every classroom teacher. Principals never want the reputation of having "weak" discipline at their schools. The public demands that schools be places of effective discipline that create environments where teachers can teach and students can learn.

DEFINING THE GOALS OF SCHOOL DISCIPLINE

What do we mean by the term *discipline?* Surely, it means more than a series of descriptive adjectives. Without a clear definition of the term, how do we recognize good discipline when we achieve it? *Webster's New World College Dictionary* (1996) defines the term as follows:

Discipline: From the Latin term *disciplina,* meaning: 1. A branch of knowledge or learning; 2. Training that develops self-control, character, orderliness or efficiency; 3. Strict control to enforce obedience; 4. Treatment that controls or punishes; 5. A system of rules.

It is interesting to note that the definitions of the term suggest that discipline can have quite different implications for schools. The component of the definition that relates to teaching seems much more positive than the components that include the negative expressions such as *punishment* and *strict control.* Those elements that involve exercising "obedience" seem more akin to what we expect while training animals than it does to working with children and youth. The definition does provide an interesting framework for discussing the role of discipline in schools.

As a Branch of Knowledge

School discipline is not usually thought of as a branch of knowledge. The study of a subject like physics, history, biology, or philosophy is a more likely example of a "discipline." Branches of knowledge usually contain research, empirical data, a certain amount of theory, and a great many experts. Most of the expertise relates to classroom rather than schoolwide discipline. Schoolwide discipline differs from classroom discipline because it focuses on practices that relate to the total operation of the school rather than a single classroom. There are few books and even fewer contemporary experts on schoolwide discipline as a research study.

The best experts in the area of schoolwide discipline are practicing school administrators. The environment in which schools operate changes so quickly that it is difficult for theorists to keep up with contemporary problems of discipline. Issues related to substance abuse, weapons, sexual harassment, dress codes, and compulsory attendance seem to change continually. Problems in schools in one part of the nation are not the same as those in other sections of the country.

Consequences for misbehavior vary according to the community in which the school is located.

As Training to Develop Self-Control

Philosophers and educators of the eighteenth and nineteenth centuries wrote and taught about discipline of the mind as though it were similar to discipline of the body. In early schools, history, science, languages, and grammar were taught as mental disciplines that required memorization, drill, practice, and, above all, dedication to the subject. The scholar acquired knowledge by stamina and diligence. Moral character was closely related to the ability of the individual to discipline himself or herself and to become "a good person" through mastery and control of urges and appetites. According to these scholars, the value of education lies not in the content of the subject being taught, but in the process of acquisition. "Through dedication and hard work, the educated person can apply the principles of self-discipline to every needed body of knowledge" (Monroe, 1918, p. 263).

Some people in our contemporary society believe that these early professors of pedagogy had a point. Perhaps the reason test scores are so low in some parts of the country is related to lack of discipline. Perhaps we need more drill and practice in addition to experiential learning. Some types of learning are hard work. There is no easy way to memorize periodic tables, conjugation of verbs, poems, or the capitals of the nations. Although modern psychology teaches us the mind is not a muscle, humans are more productive when they are able to discipline their emotions and appetites and to concentrate on a given task for a certain amount of time without interruption. Perhaps concentration and a degree of disciplined learning are areas that need to be reemphasized in schools.

School discipline can play a key role in character education. Older youth must learn that things are not always black and white, and that sometimes the good of society must be considered before the interests of any single individual. Younger children must learn that when you are living in a group, it is not always possible to get your own way. All students must learn to understand how other people feel when they are treated unjustly. Students need to be taught that they must abide by the rules if they want to receive the benefits that society has to offer.

Children and youth develop skills of socialization and moral reasoning in part through discipline practices. Child psychologists tell us that setting limits helps children feel secure. Discipline provides the modeling, rules, limits, and moral framework within which the individual develops his or her sense of adjustment to society. Without discipline, individuals have no boundaries and are left to wander aimlessly in a moral wilderness. Absolute freedom may be acceptable for philosophers but not for students who have to learn to live in the real world.

Too much has been made of "Whose moral values would you teach?" types of arguments. There are many moral values on which most people can agree. Examples are honesty, nonviolence, empathy, responsibility for our own actions, tolerance, respect for authority, respect for oneself, and loyalty to family and country. Most of these basic moral principles are taught by good teachers in their classrooms on a daily basis. We talk about teaching values as if they were something new when actually, good teachers have been teaching moral values for generations.

The word *teaching* can be directly related to the word *habits*. It is through the formation of habits that most humans are trained. There are a number of "habits" that can be internalized through school discipline practices. These basic habits include not throwing trash on the ground; arriving to work on time; not using improper language in a social setting; and showing common courtesy toward others. These may seem very elementary, but anyone visiting a modern public school will notice examples of students who have not learned or have not acquired these basic habits.

Certainly, social habits such as courtesy, punctuality, proper language, and cleanliness should be learned and emphasized in the home and are not the primary responsibility of the school. The fact of the matter is, however, that a great number of students come to school without the so-called social graces. The school is the most likely institution to fill the gap of appropriate training in social skills. The school disciplinarian has the responsibility of leadership in ensuring that all members of the school staff play a role in the daily reinforcement of appropriate social habits. It is a difficult assignment that takes patience, determination, and skill. Yet it is already being done in thousands of schools across the nation.

As Strict Control to Enforce Obedience

There is no doubt that someone needs to be in charge of our schools. As long as schools are composed of hundreds or thousands of students who are required by law to reside in an institutional setting for several hours a day, several times a week, there must be someone in control. Control does not mean being a warden at a prison. It means maintaining order and discipline. One needs only a short time at a school campus to determine whether or not someone is in control. Someone is in control of a school when

1. Students are where they are supposed to be at any given hour of the school day.

2. There are few interruptions of class time.

3. The campus is clean and free of graffiti.

4. Campus visitors are screened and required to wear a visitor's badge.

5. Communication devices are visible and readily available.

6. Supervisory personnel are visible.

7. Students, teachers, and administrators have a good working relationship.

As Treatment to Control or Punish

The terms *discipline* and *punishment* are often used in a manner where one supposedly requires the other to exist. This is not necessarily the case. The term *punishment* is usually related to some type of suffering or deprivation. Discipline is related more to teaching and self-control. To be realistic, we must admit that punishment exists because of the expectations of society. This is particularly true in schools. When students misbehave, adults expect them to be punished. The degree of punishment may depend on the community in which the school is located. For example, in the southern part of the nation, corporal punishment is much more acceptable than in other parts. In 1993, there were 613,514 instances of paddling reports in the United States. Most of those paddling cases occurred in southern states. Corporal punishment is still legal in 26 states, but there has been a 32% decline in corporal punishment in schools from 1991 to 1992, and most of that decline was in eastern and western states (Richardson, Wilcox, & Dunne, 1995). Corporal punishment may not only be accepted but expected in the Deep South, but in Rhode Island, administrators can lose their credentials if they strike a student for any reason.

Social psychologists have been telling us for decades that rehabilitation and not punishment changes negative behavior. Unfortunately, the courts and the community at large still do not see it that way. The number of men and women in prisons and jails in the United States in 1995 climbed to 1.6 million, nearly double the rate imprisoned in 1985. The United States has more people in prison than any other industrialized nation (U.S. Department of Justice, 1995).

Punishment in our culture is tied primarily to supporting the norms of the majority of persons who abide by the rules. Schools suspend students not so much to improve the behavior of the students who do not follow the rules, but to reinforce the norms for proper behavior set forth by the adult community.

When we enforce norms, we must be sensitive to both what we are and what we are not doing. Enforcing social norms through punishment may be necessary to protect the majority from the actions of sociopaths, psychopaths, and moral misfits. Punishment, however, may not be the best way to teach self-discipline. What we are after in self-discipline is not fear of retribution but, rather, a habitual response pattern. This response pattern is formed through modeling, demands, restrictions, and limitations. We want students to behave not because they are frightened, but because they respect authority and desire to belong. Students need to believe that being a member of the student body of a specific school is a good thing. It is something they want to do; they want to belong. This is an especially powerful drive for most teenagers. Excessive punishment can negate and confuse some of the positive goals we are trying to achieve. It can emphasize that the school and the world at large is a negative place.

It is important to stress that students cannot learn self-discipline if they are removed from the very environment where instruction is to occur. There is some research that indicates that punishment actually stops the learning process. Excessive punishment may create a situation in which the offender holds such a grudge against the institution that anger can supersede any need to belong (Bandura, 1973). We know that suspension is a common punishment used in schools when students fail to abide by rules, but there is little research to support out-of-school suspension as an effective deterrent to misbehavior (Moles, 1990; Stevens, 1983).

As a System of Rules

Rules are crucial for good discipline. It is wonderful to imagine a utopia where rules would not be necessary in the society—and certainly not in schools—because of the degree of self-discipline shown by those who live there. If students are to transfer their school experience to living in adult society, they must learn to live with rules and laws. There are many kinds of rules and laws to which students must attend. Chapter 2 of this book is devoted entirely to rules and the ways that effective school administrators have used rules to teach justice in their schools.

PROVIDING LEADERSHIP FOR FAIR AND JUST DISCIPLINE PRACTICES

Webster's definition helped us think about what the term *discipline* means to us in terms of goals and objectives. If the objective of discipline for a school is strictly control, then perhaps school boards should employ police officers as school disciplinarians. Their training is probably more conducive to control, and they probably can do a better job. If the objective of school discipline is instruction, then educators have a legitimate and logical role to play. The formation of rules, the isolation of socially acceptable habits, the enforcement of certain acceptable community moral standards, and the implementation of practices that demonstrate our system of justice require the services of a professionally trained educator.

As a group, administrators responsible for school discipline are doing an excellent job of administering our schools. Most are skilled in the profession and find the role of school disciplinarian to be challenging and one of the best jobs in education. They can be exhausted at times by petty trivia. They can also be frustrated by teachers and parents who do not do their jobs. It should not be their responsibility to be a classroom disciplinarian. Parents and teachers must fulfill their roles so school administrators can provide leadership and direction for schools. School disciplinarians, especially, have the opportunity to be leaders of justice and fairness, a task that takes time, total school involvement, and a great deal of energy.

USING A JUSTICE ISSUES SCHOOL CHECKLIST

Form 1 (Justice Issues School Checklist) at the end of this chapter provides school administrators with a way to evaluate where their leadership may be needed with regard to discipline practices. The form identifies 25 school discipline practices and fairness issues. The form can be distributed to teachers, student councils, and parent groups. The results should be collected and scored by a special committee appointed by the school administrator in charge of discipline. Those areas rated "Almost never" and "Some of the time" by at least half those who complete the survey need to be the focus of the committee. Some schools call the committee the School Justice Task Force. The committee needs to meet on a regular basis to find ways to improve identified areas of concern. The committee might establish one school year as the time needed to improve the situation. A second survey can be taken at the end of the year to determine how much progress has been made. The school administrator in charge of discipline is responsible for providing the leadership in the areas of concern, but the involvement of the entire school community is necessary to make real change.

Form 1   Justice Issues School Checklist

Justice Issues School Checklist

Use the scale to rate your school in each of the school justice areas described.

Almost all the time	Most of the time	Some of the time	Almost never
4	3	2	1

1. Boys and girls receive equal treatment by teachers. _____

2. Girls and boys receive equal consequences for the same offense. _____

3. The consequences of disobeying school rules are distributed in writing to students and parents. _____

4. School rules are periodically reevaluated for clarity and appropriateness by a committee of administrators, teachers, parents, and students. _____

5. Grading practices are fair. _____

6. Classroom discipline practices are fair and consistent. _____

7. Students with disabilities receive fair and equal treatment. _____

8. Students speaking limited English receive fair and equal treatment. _____

9. A reasonable attempt is made to keep drugs and weapons off the school campus. _____

10. Students have an opportunity to express themselves at school board meetings. _____

11. The opportunity to attend school is not restricted because of race, religion, ethnic group, or physical disability. _____

12. Student searches comply with school district, state, and federal laws. _____

13. Persons who do not belong on the school campus are kept off. _____

14. School facilities are safe and clean. _____

15. Students understand their rights under the law. _____

16. Students and parents feel free to question school rules and district policies. _____

17. School compulsory attendance laws are enforced. _____

18. Students are not discriminated against because of their race. _____

19. Students are not discriminated against because of their religion. _____

20. Students are not discriminated against because of their gender. _____

21. Students are not discriminated against because of their ethnic origin. _____

22. Students are not discriminated against because of their clothing or appearance. _____

23. School officials make a sincere attempt to communicate with parents and guardians when necessary. _____

24. Staff assigned to campus security are well informed about school discipline and treat students fairly. _____

25. Students involved in suspension or expulsion proceedings are given an opportunity for a fair hearing. _____

2

Developing Good School Rules and a Student Code of Conduct

As long as large numbers of people live and work together in close proximity, there will always need to be a system of rules. Some rules are initiated by elected governing bodies, while others are established by select committees. Generally, in our society, we try to refrain from rules that are made by a single individual. Most often, rules are written down and have various names such as "codes," "laws," "statutes," "regulations," or "policies." Regardless of what they are called, the purpose of written rules is to provide consistency of application and equality of treatment. Written rules exist primarily to ensure that "fairness" or "justice" exists.

It is important for schools to teach students about the importance of rules. It is also important to administer schools in accordance with written rules, so that students can learn that they are living in a society ruled by laws, and that no single individual can determine his or her own fate. As much as maturity and age permit, schools should be models of democracy. Children and youth must understand that rules and regulations exist to provide for the orderly operation of the school. They should also understand that it is possible to have a system of rules without infringing on the basic rights of all those who attend and work in the school.

There is no better place to teach fairness and justice than in schools. It is in schools that students are introduced to the fact that they have rights, privileges, and responsibilities under the law. It is in schools that students learn that laws are established for the benefit of the common good. It is in schools that students benefit from the fair application of rules.

Students must learn that there are a number of different kinds of rules or laws that they must obey as citizens of society. Each of those kinds of laws has its source in a different institution.

Each of the institutions that make school laws is established by elected bodies (e.g., state legislators) or by interpretations of individuals who are appointed by elected officials (e.g., school district superintendents or school principals). It is important for students to understand that when they become adults, they may participate in helping to make the rules.

There are a number of sources for school rules and laws, some of which are the following:

The U.S. Constitution and the Bill of Rights. Examples are due process rights, free speech, and freedom from discrimination due to race, language spoken, gender, religion, ethnic origin, or sexual preference.

Federal laws and regulations. Examples are federal statutes related to special education, gun control, drugs, and possession or use of explosive devices.

State constitutions. Examples are state statutes relating to compulsory attendance, suspension, expulsion, safety, and teacher credentialing.

Local board of education policies. Examples are requirements for graduation, open or closed campuses, the length of the school day, and student dress regulations.

LEGAL REQUIREMENT FOR LOCAL SCHOOL RULES

Local school rules provide a major opportunity to teach students about the importance of rules and laws. Most schools provide students and parents with a written list of rules by which students must abide while at school. Most schools call this written list of rules a student code of conduct. Many states now require that schools file a copy of their student code of conduct with the superintendent of schools of the school district in which the school is located. Student codes of conduct have become more than a simple list of "do's" and "don'ts." Student codes of conduct satisfy legal requirements concerning written notification of students and parents. Schools that do not have written codes of conduct may be asked to prove in a court of law how their students were informed of the consequences of misbehavior.

State regulations concerning written codes of conduct differ slightly, but there is a certain amount of similarity of form and content. California's Education Code (Section 35291.5) is typical of many of the state requirements concerning written codes of conduct. It states

a) On or before December 1, 1987, and at least every 4 years thereafter, each public school, in accordance with the requirements of this section, shall adopt rules and procedures on school discipline applicable to the school. The school discipline rules and procedures shall be consistent with any applicable policies adopted by the governing board and state statutes governing school discipline. In developing these rules and procedures, each school shall solicit the participation, views, and advice of one representative selected by each of the following groups:

1. Parents

2. Teachers

3. School administrators

4. School security personnel, if any

5. For junior high schools and high schools, pupils enrolled in the school

Meetings for the development of the rules and procedures should be developed and held within the school's existing resources, during non-classroom hours, and on normal school days.

The final version of the rules and procedures on school discipline with attendant regulations shall be adopted by a panel comprised of the principal of the school, or his or her designee, and a representative selected by classroom teachers employed at the school.

It shall be the duty of each employee of the school to enforce the rules and procedures on school discipline adopted under this section.

b) The governing board of each school district shall prescribe procedures to provide written notice to continuing pupils at each school year and to transfer pupils at the time of their enrollment in the school and to their parents or guardians regarding the school discipline rules and procedures adopted pursuant to subdivision (a).

c) Each school shall file a copy of its school discipline rules and procedures with the district superintendent of schools and governing board on or before January 1, 1988.

d) The governing board may review, at an open meeting, the approved school discipline rules and procedures for consistency with governing board policy and state statutes. (School Rules and Procedures, 1987)

Most states do not regulate what goes into a student code of conduct because local circumstances influence the scope and nature of school rules.

Some schools may have rules relating to riding horses to school or where to store skiing equipment. Other schools may have rules relating to gang attire or the use of pagers and cellular telephones. State legislatures wisely determined that aside from state and federal laws relating to drugs, weapons, sexual harassment, assault and battery, and so on, school rules should be primarily local.

Some districts with several high schools may use the same student code of conduct for all high schools in the district. This policy may be expedient and may ensure that discipline requirements are consistent throughout the district. However, this does not allow for each staff and student body to help make rules to govern themselves. There is learning and a buy-in for students when they help make good school rules. Students are more likely to obey rules that they have had some role in making. There is also the learning that takes place when school rules are revised and parents, students, security personnel, and teachers have an opportunity to become involved in the rule-making or rule-revising process.

Total school involvement in rule making is crucial to the reputation of the school as a democratic institution. Schools are also somewhat proprietary institutions by nature, and those who attend or work at the school want to feel that they have contributed to making their school a special place. It is easy to understand how some districts may want all schools in the district to have the same code of conduct, but consistency between schools in a district must be measured against the disadvantages. The disadvantage is that a districtwide student code of conduct negates local school and community involvement in the rule-making process. District codes of conduct do not take advantage of the opportunity to improve the school's reputation as a democratic institution that is sensitive to the views of the community.

Most student codes of conduct contain what might be called "protect your tail" kinds of rules. They can be direct quotes from state or federal laws or district policies. In many cases, the quotes contain language that is too difficult for most students, as well as many parents, to understand. The law is quoted in the code because it serves as proof that students and parents were notified of the law, statute, or policy. This is especially true of laws related to weapons, drugs, or alcohol possession. "Protect your tail" types of legalese quotes can be made more effective when they are paraphrased into rules that students and parents can readily understand.

WHAT MAKES A GOOD SCHOOL RULE?

How do you evaluate what makes a good school rule? Many schools revise their student code of conduct at least every other year. The following exercise (Form 2) is intended to assist school committees when they have the opportunity to revise or create a student code of conduct.

Form 2   What Makes a Good School Rule?

What Makes a Good School Rule?

What do you think some of the criteria should be for good school rules? Have someone write your committee's list on the board. Then do the following activity to determine if you have left a criterion for good school rule-making off your list.

The following are 10 rules made by 10 fictitious authority figures. Divide your committee into groups of four to six people. Have each group take one or two of the scenarios listed here and determine:

a. Why did the person make the rule?

b. What is wrong with the rule?

c. How can you improve the rule to help the rule maker achieve his or her purpose?

1. Mr. Johnson, a high school principal, was upset with the number of fights occurring on his school campus, so he made the following rule: "Any student caught fighting on school campus will spend every lunch period and 2 hours after school in a detention room until graduation."

2. Ms. Robertson, a middle school teacher, was concerned with the number of students coming to school under the influence of drugs, so she made the following rule: "Students coming to my class in any way vulnerable to the deleterious effects of an illegal substance will be sent immediately to the principal's office."

3. There were too many students being sent to the office for disciplinary reasons, so the principal made a rule that said: "All students should behave themselves and do the correct thing."

4. Dr. Watson, the superintendent of schools, was concerned about the weapons problem in his school district, so he made the following rule: "Any student caught with a weapon in his or her possession will be sent immediately to juvenile prison."

5. The governor of the state was concerned about the number of student attacks on teachers, so he made the following rule: "Any student who attacks a teacher will be publicly whipped."

6. To reduce alcohol abuse among students in the district, the school board made the following rule: "It will be against board policy for students to purchase alcohol in off-campus liquor stores."

7. To help stop the number of truancies on campus, the student council made the following rule: "Students who are truant to class will no longer be allowed to participate in athletics or school dances."

8. Ms. Fredericks, the assistant principal, was concerned about girls' being late to class due to primping in the restroom, so she made the following rule: "Girls late to class for any reason must remain after school for one hour for each minute late to class."

9. The chief of police was concerned about the number of thefts from garages being made by students walking to and from school, so he made the following rule: "Students walking to and from school must walk on the sidewalk along the curb, or they will be arrested."

10. Mr. Matthews, a high school teacher, was concerned about the amount of cheating going on in his class, so he made the following rule: "Students caught cheating on a test will be expelled from school."

Rule	Weakness	Rule Should Have Said
1.		
2.		
3.		
4.		
5.		
6.		
7.		
8.		
9.		
10.		

After each group has completed its answers, reconvene to the original committee. Select someone from each group to read the scenario reviewed and give the group's answers to the three evaluation questions. Record each group's answer as to what was wrong with the rule proposed by the authority figure in each scenario on a blackboard or flip chart. After each of the 10 scenarios is completed by the groups, review your original list of good rule criteria with the committee. Are there some criteria that are not on the list that are suggested by the group activity?

WHAT TO INCLUDE IN A STUDENT CODE OF CONDUCT

The Michigan State Board of Education has made some excellent recommendations for school districts to keep in mind when developing school regulations:

1. The policy must provide notice of what conduct is prohibited or permitted;

2. The rules must be reasonable and understandable to the average student;

3. The rules must be rationally related to a valid educational purpose;

4. The rules must be precise so as not to prohibit constitutionally protected activities;

5. The policy must provide students with notice of potential consequences for violating specific rules;

6. The type of punishment specified in the policy must be within the expressed or implied authority of the school district to use;

7. The punishment must be of reasonable severity in relation to the seriousness of the conduct or the number of times the misconduct was committed;

8. A copy of the rules and procedures must be disseminated to all students. (Michigan State Department of Education, 1992)

A MODEL STUDENT CODE OF CONDUCT

After reviewing hundreds of student codes of conduct from schools throughout the United States, the author has compiled a model code that school administrators and others may use for comparative purposes when writing or revising a student code of conduct for their school. The following is the suggested format for a model code.

Introductory Statement

The introductory statement can be a short statement by the principal, the superintendent of schools, the student body president, or the president of a parent organization. The obvious disadvantage of an introductory statement is that it has to be changed as the people change.

Statement of Student Responsibilities

Usually, these statements are general in nature and emphasize the following types of student responsibilities:

- Responsibility to attend school on a regular basis and to be on time
- Responsibility to complete all academic work as assigned
- Responsibility to bring the appropriate tools to class
- Responsibility to obey school rules and state and federal laws
- Responsibility to respect the rights of others
- Responsibility for your own actions
- Responsibility to use appropriate language
- Responsibility to respect school property
- Responsibility to vote in student body elections
- Responsibility to dress appropriately for school and to abide by the rules of modesty, safety, and cleanliness

Statement of Student Rights

As many schools do *not* include this section as do include it. Because we are teaching about school discipline and justice in schools, it seems appropriate to include it.

- The right to an education
- The right to due process of law in cases of expulsion
- The right to freedom of speech and expression
- The right to privacy and free association
- The right to equal protection
- The right to petition grievances
- The right to attend a safe and drug-free school
- The right to not be discriminated against

Statement Describing Student Privileges

Students need to be reminded in the student code of conduct that the following kinds of activities are not student rights:

- Graduation exercises
- Participation in athletics
- Participation in afterschool activities such as band, drama, clubs, and so on
- Senior all-night parties
- Eighth-grade parties
- Possession of a locker

Clear List of Violations of School Rules

There is a great deal of debate as to whether the consequences should be included after each rule in a student code of conduct. In our courts of law, except for parking violations, we do not list consequences. Consequences are generally left up to either the judge or the jury. Can the role of the administrator in charge of discipline be considered the same as that of a judge? In reality, that is what happens in most schools. Some courts have said that schools must spell out what kinds of discipline may be used for specific infractions. In most states, indicating the range of possible disciplinary responses is probably adequate. This provides some room for judgment on the part of those persons who assign consequences for misbehavior.

In a few schools across the nation, peer or student courts are used to assign consequences for minor types of misbehavior, such as littering, tardiness, and swearing. Peer courts have been very effective, and the recidivism rate for misbehavior occurring by students who have been involved with peer courts is very low. Peer courts take a great deal of time and need to involve lawyers and judges to be effective. Not all school administrators have that kind of time. Student courts are discussed in greater detail in Chapter 3.

In some codes, the actual federal law, state statute, or board policy section number or language is quoted after the rule. This is especially effective in relation to the laws regarding possession of marijuana, definition of a weapon, definition of a gang, registration of automobiles, off-campus regulations, gambling, and damage to school property.

Recently, some schools have asked their school districts to define sexual harassment so that it can be included in their code. Specific citations are not listed because of the differences in state and local laws regarding discipline.

Examples of rule violations and commonly applied consequences are listed in the following table. Please note that the consequences are not necessarily recommendations from the author but represent a consensus of consequences listed in more than 100 student codes of conduct from all over the United States.

Violation	Consequence
Cheating	Automatic failure of the test in question and 3 hours of after school detention
Fighting	Automatic 3-day suspension of both parties involved
Assault	Automatic 5-day suspension or possible recommendation to the Board of Education for expulsion
Theft	3-day suspension
Smoking	3-day suspension
Defiance of authority	1-day suspension
Damaging school property	3-day suspension and cost of restoring property
Possession or sale of illegal substances, weapons, or explosive devices	Automatic recommendation to the Board of Education for expulsion

Violation	Consequence
Leaving campus without permission	2-day suspension
Littering	After school suspension and cleanup detail
Disruption of school time	2-day suspension
Sexual harassment	3-day suspension and an apology
Gambling	3-day suspension
Being under the influence of an illegal substance, including alcohol	3-day suspension, one semester probation, and removal from extracurricular activities
Forgery	2-day suspension unless it is a school document, in which case it can be a recommendation to the Board of Education for expulsion
Arson	Automatic recommendation to the Board of Education for expulsion

NOTE: When the term *suspension* is used in some schools this may mean in-school rather than out-of-school suspension.

Explanation of Student Due Process Rights

Codes of student conduct should include a complete explanation of the procedural rights that students have in cases of suspension or expulsion. They should be reviewed annually by the district's counsel in light of changing legal requirements. Including due process rights satisfies both instructional and legal purposes. It is important for students to know that they have due process rights and that the school makes an effort to enforce them. A student code of conduct satisfies a legal due process requirement for schools, and the district and individual schools should make every effort to word its code as precisely as possible. The following is an example of student due process rights that could be included in a student code of conduct:

When students are suspended or recommended for expulsion, they are entitled to the following due process rights:

1. To know what the charges are against them and the evidence supporting the charges.

2. The opportunity for a hearing at which they can defend themselves. A parent or other representative can be present at that hearing. The hearing should occur as close as possible to the time the offense was committed.

Students should note that due process is not required for decisions related to athletics, marching band, cheerleading, or other extracurricular activities.

Information to Help Explain
the Student Code of Conduct

It is often necessary to explain what terms mean to students in plain language. The following are helpful examples of language taken from various discipline codes:

Respect for Others. The XYZ School District affirms its policy that all students and adults will be treated equally and respectfully and refrain from the use of slurs against any person on the basis of race, language, color, sex, religion, handicap, national origin, immigration status, age, sexual orientation, or political belief.

Sexual Harassment. The XYZ High School District will not condone, permit, or tolerate sexual harassment of employees or students in any manner whatsoever. Persons engaging in such harassment may be subject to discipline up to and including discharge or expulsion. Sexual harassment is defined as unwarranted verbal or physical sexual advances, sexually explicit derogatory statements, or sexually discriminatory remarks made by someone in the education environment that are offensive or objectionable to the student, that cause the student discomfort or humiliation, or that interfere with the student's performance.

Visitors. A visitor is any person not a student, parent or guardian of a student, or an employee of the school district. All visitors should report to the reception area upon coming on campus during school hours. School hours are defined as one hour before school begins and one hour after school ends. All persons classified as visitors must receive permission from a school administrator before coming on campus. All unauthorized visitors are subject to arrest and a fine.

Gang Dress. The Board prohibits the presence of any apparel, jewelry, accessory, notebook, or manner of grooming that, by virtue of its color, arrangement, trademark, or any other attribute, denotes membership in gangs that advocate drug use, violence, or disruptive behavior. This policy shall be applied at the principal's discretion, after consultation with the superintendent of schools, as the need for it arises at individual school sites.

A Gang. A group of individuals who may or may not claim control over a certain territory in the community and who engage, either individually or collectively, in violent or other forms of illegal behavior.

Assault. A violent physical attack or threat of physical attack.

Suspension. The temporary removal of a student from a classroom or a school campus for refusing to abide by the rules and regulations by which the institution is administered.

Expulsion. The permanent removal of a student from the schools of the school district for exhibiting behavior that is detrimental to the safety, welfare, and morals of students or of school personnel in the school or school district.

Habitually Disruptive Behavior. When a student has caused a disruption in a classroom, on school grounds, on vehicles, or at school events on more than one occasion.

Illegal Substance. Any product that can be ingested into the body that is determined by law to be against the law to possess or to ingest. (Each state has its own definition.)

Appropriate Dress. Appropriate dress is deemed to be clothing and appearance that is safe, modest, and clean. Safety refers specifically to appropriate shoes. Modesty refers to clothing that covers the body in a fashion that is not a distraction to others. Modesty also means that there is no lettering or pictures portrayed that could be deemed offensive to public morals. Cleanliness means personal hygiene and clothing that is not distracting to others due to smell or appearance.

Electronic Device. Apparatus used for purposes of communication or entertainment that is detrimental to the learning environment.

Closed Campus. All persons leaving the school grounds during the school day must have a pass.

Habitual Truant. A student who is absent from school for more than three times without a legitimate excuse.

Extortion. Obtaining or attempting to obtain money or property from an unwilling person or forcing an individual to act by either physical force or intimidation (threat).

Insubordination. Knowingly refusing to comply with reasonable school rules, refusal to identify self, or to follow directions of school personnel.

Arson. Setting fire, or attempting to set fire, to a school building or property located on school grounds or any property belonging to, rented by, or on loan to the school district, or property (including automobiles) of persons employed by the school or in attendance at the school.

A Weapon. Any object that can cause serious injury to a person when used in an unlawful manner.

Local School Rules

Each school may have special rules in its student code of conduct that are different from those of other schools, rules that relate to do's and don'ts. Some of those local school rules might concern

- Use or possession of cell phones on school campus
- Parking areas (for cars, bikes, motorcycles, skis, horses, or skateboards)
- Out of bounds areas
- Carrying a student ID card
- Hats in the classroom or on campus
- Insignias of sports teams on jackets
- Wearing shorts on campus
- Wearing curlers, hairnets, or bandannas
- Wearing dangling hoop earrings
- Failure to attend Saturday school or afterschool detention
- Bringing animals on campus
- Use of lockers
- Baggy pants and hip huggers
- Sunglasses
- Tattoos
- Sandals
- Pacifiers or baby bottles
- Spikes or chains
- Gloves when not appropriate to the weather
- Belts with insignias

Warnings

Most student codes of conduct also contain certain warnings that are not as much disciplinary as they are safety related. Examples are

- Do not bring valuable jewelry or large amounts of money to school.
- Be certain to lock your locker and protect your belongings while at school.
- Do not wear overly loose clothing or long hair while engaged in operating machinery.
- Do not get into cars with strangers.
- Be certain you have a hall pass if you are out of class.
- Park in authorized zones or your car will be towed.

- Listen to the daily bulletin and announcements carefully for special information.
- Be certain you have permission to take medication while on school grounds.
- Follow all special athletic, band, or club requirements that relate to discipline.

Athletic or Marching Band Code of Conduct

Many coaching staffs or band directors insist on having a separate code of conduct for their athletes or band members. Sometimes these codes can be too strict and violate the attempts to teach through good school rules. The assistant principal in charge of discipline must retain the right to review all such codes and to suggest changes where necessary.

Using the Words "May," "Can," or "Will"

The word *may* obviously softens a rule but leaves the door open for the application of consequences. Most often *may* is used in rules that apply to privileges, for example: "Seniors may lose their right to participate in graduation exercises if . . ." Phrases such as *can result in* can be used in situations where the administrator in charge wants to be able to have some options. Many schools are using *can result in* listed consequences for fighting. Sometimes both parties are not equally guilty in instigating the fight, and the administrator may want to punish one participant more than the other.

The use of the term *will* is as close to zero tolerance as you can get. If the term is used, the consequence had better be firm and consistently applied.

List of Positive Rewards

There is a growing tendency to list rewards for outstanding behavior in a student code of conduct. Examples are

- No final exams for students who have perfect attendance
- Pizza parties for homerooms with the best attendance
- Special T-shirts for students who are special examples of good citizenship

CONCLUSION

Form 3 (Checklist for a Student Code of Conduct) offers a good way to review what has been discussed in this chapter. This checklist is recommended by the Department of Education in Florida for all school districts in the state (Florida State Department of Education, 1993).

Form 3   Checklist for a Student Code of Conduct

Checklist for a Student Code of Conduct

Element in student code of conduct	Yes	No
Review Process		
• Annual review and update of policy conducted	___	___
• Parents, staff, and students are involved in development, review, revision, and implementation of code	___	___
• Consequences for all violations clearly outlined	___	___
• All behavioral expectations appear in the code	___	___
• Annual review of counseling and referral procedures and programs conducted	___	___
• Code of conduct developed and carried out to meet all federal and state civil rights, equity, and antidiscrimination laws	___	___
• Unenforced behaviors/violations removed from code	___	___
• Trivial violations removed from code	___	___
Code Enforcement		
• Annual review conducted for consistency, fairness, and data sources	___	___
• Process established for hearings and review of disciplinary actions	___	___
Notification/Training About Code		
• Code of conduct provided to students and parents every year	___	___
• Sign-off sheet maintained to verify receipt of code of conduct by students and parents	___	___

Administrators and all those involved in the school discipline process may want to review their code to see if they have included the elements recommended by practitioners and experts in the state of Florida.

Florida's checklist goes on to list requirements for certification for Federal Drug-Free Schools Funding and a state-mandated reporting list for serious behavioral incidents. Not all states have such reporting forms. The importance of having a well-thought-out and up-to-date student code of conduct cannot be overemphasized. The code is the foundation on which discipline procedures are built. It is crucial that the student body and the community do not see discipline as the domain of a single individual who makes the rules as he or she goes along. If schools are to be seen as democratic institutions that reflect the norms and values of society, then rules must be written down and reviewed with students and, if possible, with parents, as often as possible.

Certainly, teachers must have a thorough knowledge of what school rules exist, how they are formed, and why they exist.

3

Setting Consequences for Breaking Rules

S tudents who disobey school rules do so for a number of reasons, including lack of self-control, the need for attention, social maladjustment, lack of moral training in the home, maliciousness, or poor adult modeling. It should be emphasized that most students attend school without the need for consequences for misbehavior because they rarely do anything wrong. The number of students who get into trouble with school authorities varies from school to school, but most educators would agree it runs between 3% and 5% of the student population.

The author has been in schools where approximately 50% of the students are suspended during the school year. This is a rarity but is more likely to occur in urban schools with a great deal of poverty in the community.

Statistics demonstrate that most of the students who attend our schools rarely need to see a school administrator for disciplinary reasons. School administrators in charge of discipline are quick to remind us, however, that they generally spend 90% of their time on the 5% who misbehave. Misbehaving students take a great deal of time and require both patience and determination on the part of school administrators, teachers, and counselors.

What consequences exist for that 5% who cannot seem to abide by the rules? Schools have different consequences for different kinds of offenses. Consequences for student misbehavior can be divided into three different categories:

1. Consequences for violating classroom rules

2. Consequences for violating state and federal laws

3. Consequences for violating campus rules outlined in the student code of conduct

Each category can be examined separately.

TEACHERS' RESPONSIBILITY FOR CLASSROOM DISCIPLINE

Many principals draw on their own experiences as instructional leaders to assist beginning and other teachers with classroom management problems. Classroom teachers, however, have the direct responsibility for maintaining discipline and order in their classrooms. Teachers need to establish the rules necessary so that the classroom atmosphere is conducive to learning. Generally, classroom rules include topics that relate to the following types of behavior for students:

- Students will attend class regularly unless they are ill or an emergency occurs.
- Students will come to school on time every day.
- Students will bring the proper tools to class, including a pencil, paper, books, and required items.
- Students will treat others with courtesy and respect.
- Students will not speak until called on by the teacher unless the rules of the classroom allow for free interaction between students.
- Students will sit in their assigned seats.
- Students will not leave the class without permission until the class is over.
- Students will not bring food, drinks, gum, hats, or other distractions to the classroom without the permission of the teacher.
- Students will actively participate in learning activities assigned by the teacher.

Consequences for failing to abide by one or more of these rules are the responsibility of the classroom teacher. Consequences can include the following:

1. Verbal reprimand

2. Changing a student's seat assignment

3. Extra assignments to be done at home

4. Afterschool detention

5. A call to a parent or a parent conference

6. Notation on the grade card

Generally, minor violations of classroom rules do not require the attention of a school administrator unless the student refuses to respect the authority of the teacher. Most schools recommend that classroom discipline be kept separate from academic progress. At times, however, discipline problems will affect the student's grades on tests, homework, or daily participation.

School administrators need to be careful not to take the responsibility for enforcing classroom discipline away from teachers. Teachers must know that they are expected to control what happens in their classrooms, and only in extraordinary cases should an administrator be called in for assistance.

Referrals to the school disciplinarian are a last-resort option available to teachers for students who continually refuse to abide by classroom rules. Schools need a standardized form for teachers to use when it becomes necessary to refer a student to an administrator. Copies of the referral should be sent to parents, coaches, band directors, and others who have a special interest in the student offender. Most schools have a Discipline Referral Form that generally looks something like Form 4.

VIOLATIONS OF FEDERAL AND STATE LAWS AND SCHOOL DISCIPLINE

Consequences for student violations of state or federal laws on school campuses should be stated in the student code of conduct, which was described in Chapter 2.

Breaking a federal law on a school campus is a serious offense and necessitates involvement of law enforcement agencies and, in most cases, recommendation for expulsion from the school district. Examples are possessing or discharging a firearm on a school campus, selling or possessing narcotics on a school campus, and serious cases of sexual harassment. Violations of a state law on a school campus can result in suspension or, for repeat offenses, in a recommendation for expulsion.

Zero tolerance is a term that is used more and more frequently by state legislatures and generally refers to violations related to weapons, drugs, and assaults against students or school employees. Zero tolerance means that there is no leeway in deciding what to do with the student who commits a certain type of serious offense, and that students found guilty will be expelled from the school district regardless of any extenuating circumstances. The term underscores the concern state legislatures are feeling in relation to certain types of problems being experienced by schools throughout the nation.

There are differences in the way state legislatures deal with suspension and expulsion in state statutes. In California, for instance, Section 48900 of the California Education Code states that "pupils may not be suspended from school or recommended for expulsion unless the superintendent or the principal of the school in which the pupil is enrolled determines that the pupil has" committed one of 11 specific offenses (School District

Form 4   Discipline Referral Form

Discipline Referral Form

Student name: _____   Date: _____

Classroom period or time of referral: _____

Reason for referral: _____

_____

_____

_____

_____

Teacher's name:

- -

Action taken:

Student/teacher conference _____   Administrator conference _____

Parent conference _____   Referral to counselor _____

Issuance of warning _____   After school detention _____

Saturday school _____   Out-of-school suspension _____

Other:

Administrator's name:

- -

Copy (copies) sent to:

Parent(s) _____   Counselor _____   Teacher _____

Records Office _____   Athletic Director _____   Band Director _____

Guidelines for Suspension and Expulsion, 1986). In Colorado, a statute encourages parents, guardians, or legal custodians "to attend class with the pupil for a period of time specified by the suspending authority." (Colorado Revised Statutes, 1974). In Florida, a statute states that "school boards are encouraged to include . . . alternatives to expulsion and suspension such as in-school suspension, assignment to second-chance schools, and guidelines on identification and referral of students to alcohol and substance abuse treatment agencies" (Title XVI, 1995). Additional information directly related to laws relating to suspension and expulsion will be found in Chapters 4 and 5.

CONSEQUENCES FOR VIOLATING SCHOOL RULES OUTLINED IN THE STUDENT CODE OF CONDUCT

In cases of violations of school rules, school administrators have the most latitude. Consequences used by school administrators for violations of school rules generally follow a pattern. Generally, the first offense is a warning and involves some type of reprimand. If the offense is repeated, the consequence elevates. Breaking school rules is minor in comparison with breaking state or federal laws on a school campus. Violating school rules can become serious when it involves repeated offenses of fighting, continual defiance of school authorities, or forgery of school forms. For most school rule offenses, however, the offense requires a consequence that is appropriate to teach a lesson of self-discipline to the student offender and that provides a broad array of alternatives.

PRESCRIPTIVE DISCIPLINE STRATEGIES

When a student violates a school rule, it is often due to making a poor choice. School rule violations differ from violations of state or federal law on a school campus because they are germane to the proper operation of the school but usually do not threaten the safety or welfare of the student body as a whole. In most cases, school rule violators are immature but not necessarily malicious. They may be a "pain in the neck," but they are generally fairly good people who have to be reminded that they need to grow up a little.

Different students disobey school rules for different reasons and may therefore need different consequences. School administrators should have a variety of strategies for dealing with students who have to be brought back on track. Following is a list of consequences that can be called "prescriptive discipline strategies" because of the need to administer different strategies to different students depending on their personalities, the seriousness of the offense, and the recidivism involved. The strategies are not necessarily recommended for use in any type of priority basis. Good judgment and a certain amount of pragmatism are needed by the school administrator who selects the appropriate consequence for each individual school-rule violator. The goal is not to punish but to teach self-discipline through consequences.

The Verbal Reprimand

Verbal reprimand is a common consequence used by both parents and educators for minor infractions. Generally used as a reminder, a verbal reprimand is frequently used for throwing rocks or seed pods, littering, frequent classroom disruptions, tardiness, being out of class, improper clothing, or use of foul language.

A verbal reprimand should be different from nagging and should have the following four objectives:

1. **Focus on a clear goal as to what is expected.** It should not be stated in generalities such as "Behave yourself" or "Try to be good." The reprimand should make it clear to the students that their behavior is not appropriate and will not be tolerated. There will be a more serious consequence if the misbehavior continues.

2. **Focus on issues, not personalities.** The fact that the student does not like a particular teacher or student is not the issue. The issue is the misbehavior, and it cannot continue.

3. **Focus on the present, not the past.** The issue at hand is here and now, not yesterday or tomorrow. Students need to understand that promises are not good enough; they just need to do better next time.

4. **Focus on consequences.** Ask the student the question: "If everyone or even a large number of other students did the same type of thing you did, what would be the result?" Use reasoning, and if you are not getting through, then use a little anger even if it is feigned. Show the student that you feel strongly about the misbehavior.

The Parent Contact

Parents should be the administrator's best friends when it comes to student discipline. Telephone calls to parents should be frequent and common. The administrator must assume, until proven otherwise, that parents want their children to do well in school and to comply with school rules. Parents need to be called at work if necessary to ensure prompt action. Some conscientious school administrators call parents in the evening if that is the only time they can be reached. Except in cases of suspension or expulsion, parents usually are quite helpful. They want to help discipline their children and will usually cooperate with whatever the administrator suggests. They generally appreciate that the administrator is calling out of concern that the problem should not become more serious. Most parents appreciate the preventive nature of such a telephone call or a parent conference. In cases of suspension or expulsion, the call or parent conference may not be as pleasant. A parent who has not been notified of a forthcoming problem may become quite belligerent and angry. That is all the more reason to be certain that a telephone call or a parent conference is held at an early stage.

Experienced administrators have learned that there are a number of do's and don'ts for parent conferences. The list includes the following:

- **Do** meet with parent(s) separately from the student.
- **Don't** place the parent(s) in a position where they need to defend their child to save face.
- **Do** give the parent(s) ample time to react to what has happened.
- **Don't** bully parents.
- **Do** help the parent(s) to understand how the student's behavior may be different at school than at home.
- **Don't** assume the parent(s) know how the student acts at school.
- **Do** try to help the parent(s) understand how the school works and what the procedures are when students break school rules.
- **Don't** assume that parents understand the fundamentals of education.
- **Do** assist the parent(s) in seeking outside help if necessary.
- **Don't** make it seem that you have all the answers.
- **Do** be courteous and patient.
- **Don't** make parents(s) feel that you are short on time, even if you are.
- **Do** make your expectations regarding student behavior clear and easy to understand.
- **Don't** be fuzzy about your expectations.
- **Do** make your follow-up procedures clear.
- **Don't** make it sound like this is only a one-time occurrence.

Good Record Keeping

Good record keeping is crucial when it comes to school discipline. School records may become legal documents and can be summoned into court. It is crucial that administrators keep accurate and timely records of all conferences related to school discipline. Administrators see so many people in such a short span of time that it is difficult to keep track of whom you saw, when you saw them, and what action occurred. Form 5 (Parent Contact Form) is a suggested form for keeping track of parent contacts. Computers make storage of this type of information quite easy to maintain on a daily basis, but there may a reason to have a hard copy as well.

School Counseling Services

Using a school counselor for purposes of school discipline depends on the quality of the counseling staff and the philosophy of the school. A good counselor can sometimes be invaluable to the school disciplinarian. A good counselor can talk about learning difficulties, teacher difficulties, long-term goals, personal problems, or peer issues. Obviously, administrators in charge of discipline can talk about these same areas, but the meager time available may prevent them from conducting an appropriate counseling

Form 5   Parent Contact Form

Parent Contact Form

Name of student: _____

Grade level: _____

Name of parent(s): _____

Relationship of parent to student: _____

Telephone number: (home) _____ (work) _____

Reason for call:

Date(s) of call or contact: _____   Time of call or conference: _____

Confirmation letter sent: Date _____

Summary of conference:

session and the resultant changes that may be necessary. Many counselors will say that they have great burdens on their time as well, and that they do not have the time to deal with student disciplinary cases in addition to all their other guidance tasks. Some school counselors believe that if they are the disciplinarian, they ruin their rapport with students. The problem may lie with the way the school sees discipline. Discipline should be a vital part of the teaching/counseling process. Schools that truly have a total school discipline plan involve everyone in the process of teaching self-discipline.

Discipline should be given the same priority as any other subject area or guidance need. School guidance counselors can help keep all students on task and within the boundaries of good school rules. Counselors are in the best position to deal proactively with certain types of problems before they become more serious. Suggestions as to what a counselor can do proactively to prevent a discipline problem include the following:

- **Change teachers.** It may be that one particular teacher does not allow for a language problem or a learning difficulty, or there just may be a personality clash.
- **Change the class period.** Sometimes students do better in the morning than in the afternoon or vice versa. Try a change and see if the student does better one way or the other.
- **Take advantage of positive peers.** If possible, place the students with some positive role models. Keep them away from negative influences.
- **Consider placement in a lower-level class.** Sometimes students are not able to keep up in an academic class, and this causes them to misbehave. This is particularly true where language is a problem.
- **Consider placement in a more challenging class.** Sometimes students are bored, and they need a greater challenge.
- **Refer the student to drug counseling programs.** Inform the parent that the referral has been made.
- **Assist with educational recommendations in the Individual Educational Program** of special education students.

The Student Interview

Many administrators have found that having a student complete a student interview sheet is a helpful device. It may serve as a "time-out" activity in which the student has a chance to think about what has happened. It can also provide a "cooling-off" period for the angry student. The information section of the interview sheet can provide useful insight into how the student views the incident. A sample Student Interview Form is provided as Form 6. Administrators have found the form especially helpful, and this simple form is now being used by hundreds of schools throughout the nation. The form is usually placed in the student's cumulative folder for future reference.

Form 6   Student Interview Form

Student Interview Form

Name of student: _____

Date: _____ Time: _____

Explain the reason you are in the office.

If you were sent to the office by a teacher, counselor, administrator, or other adult for violation of school or classroom rules, write a short paragraph explaining your side of the story.

What would you like to happen as a result of your meeting with a school administrator?

Friday Reports

Some students need to establish a baseline for good attendance and correct behavior. They need to establish the baseline one step at a time over a short period prior to attempting any long-term contract. Too often, administrators make yearly contracts before the student is ready for such a long-term goal.

The short-term objective can be broken down into weeks or even days if necessary. After the student has been successful in completing a short-term goal, longer commitments can be attempted.

Teachers need to receive thanks from the school administrator for taking the time to complete the Daily Assignment Log and Weekly Behavior Contract. Obviously, this is an extra but necessary responsibility for busy teachers.

Daily Assignment Logs and Weekly Behavior Contracts are especially popular with parents. They like to see what their child was supposed to accomplish each day and week and whether the teacher believed the assignments were done correctly. They also help evaluate the degree to which their child's behavior has improved. Examples of a Daily Assignment Log and Weekly Behavior Contract are included as Forms 7 and 8.

Student Behavior Contracts

Student contracts are another effective tool available to school administrators to combat student problem behavior. Student contracts are like any other kind of contract in that they are only as effective as the commitment of the persons signing them. There must also be consequences listed in the contract. A signature means nothing unless there is some consequence attached if the signer does not abide by the agreement. It is also important to have a parent sign the contract. A sample of a Student Behavior Contract is included as Form 9.

Student Apologies

Written or spoken apologies can be effective consequences for some students. They are especially effective for the first-time offender or the student who rarely gets into trouble. The apology places individuals in an embarrassing position and forces them to think about their actions. A written apology may cause even further thinking to occur. The apology can lessen the guilt attached to the offense, which for some students is important. It may not be appropriate for hardened offenders who do not sincerely regret their behavior, but it may be appropriate for the first-time offender who needs some way to come back on the right road without being labeled as a disciplinary problem student. Once again, this is a judgment call for the school administrator.

Form 7   Daily Assignment Log

DAILY ASSIGNMENT LOG

NAME: _____ SCHOOL: _____

DATE: _____ GRADE: _____

ASSIGNMENTS	TEACHER INITIALS (When assignment is recorded properly)
SUBJECT	
SUBJECT	
SUBJECT	
SUBJECT	
SUBJECT	
SUBJECT	

DIRECTIONS:

Students: 1. Record assignments.
            2. Give log to teacher to initial at end of period.
            3. Take log home.
            4. Do homework.

Parents: 1. Supply student with new form each day.
            2. Check to make sure assignments are completed.

Form 8   Weekly Behavior Contract

WEEKLY BEHAVIOR CONTRACT

NAME: _____   SCHOOL: _____

DATE: _____   GRADE: _____

<table>
<tr><td colspan="4" align="center">POSITIVE BEHAVIORS</td></tr>
<tr><td>_____</td></tr>
<tr><td>_____</td></tr>
<tr><td>_____</td></tr>
</table>

CLASS	MONDAY	TUESDAY	WEDNESDAY	THURSDAY	FRIDAY
PARENT'S INITIALS					

Total points
per day   _____ _____ _____ _____ _____

DIRECTIONS:
Teachers: Put S (Satisfactory – 10 pts), N (Needs Improvement – 5 pts), or U (Unsatisfactory – 0 pts) for each class.

Parents: Initial the contract each day to indicate it was reviewed with the student.

_____ Points per day earn _____

_____ Points per week earn _____

Student Signature: _____

Teacher/Counselor Signature: _____

Form 9   Student Behavior Contract

Student Behavior Contract

Date: _____

To: _____
            (Name of school)

From: _____ Grade: _____
            (Name of student)

Subject: Student contract for code of conduct

In consideration of my being permitted to attend: _____,
            (Name of school)

I will, to the best of my ability, live up to the following agreement:

1. Be at school every day, be on time to my classes, stay on school grounds, have no truancies from school or classes.

2. Do all class and homework assigned each day to achieve satisfactory grades.

3. Cooperate with teachers and other students.

4. Have a positive attitude and focus on learning.

5. Show respect and courtesy and avoid fights.

6. Not smoke, drink alcohol, or use other drugs.

7. Conduct myself in such a manner that I will be a credit to my school, my home, and myself.

8.

9.

I understand that I have the rights and privileges of any other student enrolled at

_____ , as long as I maintain this
            (Name of school)

agreement. Violation of this agreement can result in the cancellation of my

enrollment at _____.
            (Name of school)

_____   _____

(Student's signature)   (Parent's signature)

_____

(Administrator's signature)

Loss of Privileges

Just as Departments of Motor Vehicles and state licensing agencies deny individuals and businesses a license for not following the rules, school administrators can deny misbehaving students certain privileges. Loss of privileges is one of the most common consequences used by parents for misbehaving children.

It is important that student rights and privileges are clearly stated in the student code of conduct. Those listed in Chapter 2 include the following:

- School attendance
- School social events
- Graduation exercises
- Extracurricular activities
- Awards of excellence or achievement

Obviously, the loss of the privilege of attending school is the most serious loss and should not be taken lightly or capriciously. Denial of school attendance should be reserved for only the most severe cases where the students are a danger to themselves or to others, are continually disruptive to the school climate, or where all other efforts to get the students to comply with school rules have failed.

Taking away a privilege that means a great deal to the student is another of those judgment calls for the school administrator. Denying a student the privilege to participate in athletics, or marching band, or walking across the stage at graduation may be denying the one thing that keeps that student in school. It does not mean we do not use denial of privileges, but once again it requires a judgment call if self-defeating outcomes are to be avoided.

Demerits

At one time, the use of demerits was a common practice for school administrators. In this system, students are automatically given a certain number of merits at the beginning of the school year, and every time they commit an infraction of rules listed in the student code of conduct, a certain number of merits are deducted. If students fall below a certain number, they are called into the office and warned. If demerits continue to be awarded, a letter automatically goes out to the parents, warning them that if the behavior continues, a suspension or other consequence may be assigned. If the misbehavior continues, a suspension or other consequence occurs.

Some of the most common criticisms of demerit systems relate to the amount of bookkeeping involved and problems in using the system for poor attendance. As a result of a demerit system, a frequently truant or tardy student may be suspended for missing school. The problem with keeping a student out of school for missing school is obvious. The place where the demerit system seems to be most effective is at the middle school. Many middle schools have found the use of a demerit system to be extremely effective because younger adolescents react more favorably toward systems that reward and punish specific behaviors, whereas older adolescents may soon learn how to manipulate a demerit system.

Afterschool Detention

Afterschool detention is one of the oldest and most commonly used consequences for student misbehavior. Few adults cannot remember being "kept afterschool," which is a form of afterschool detention. Many schools have become rather sophisticated in the way they use this consequence. Some schools require that students work on classwork in which they are having the most difficulty and that they have assignment sheets with grades attached to work completed in detention. This obviously keeps it from being a time to sleep or create minor disturbances. The detention room must be a serious place where schoolwork is to occur. Teachers who send a student to detention must provide work for the student to do. Teachers often share responsibility for afterschool detention. The fact that it is after school is a problem for some districts where teacher contracts may prevent teachers from staying after school without being paid or where students rely on a bus or other prearranged transportation for the trip home.

Saturday School

Saturday school has some of the same requirements as afterschool detention. Effective Saturday schools require teacher assignments with grades attached. They also require that students not be allowed to sleep or conduct themselves in a nonserious manner. Some districts are able to collect average daily attendance funds from the state for Saturday school. This pays for the cost of the teacher and the cost of the room. Studies have shown that the grades of students assigned to Saturday school improve over those suspended from school (Duke, 1990).

Temporary Suspension From a Single Class

A temporary suspension from a single class may provide an opportunity for the students to understand how serious their actions have become. It is used to both get the student's attention and in some cases provide a "time-out" period for both student and teacher. At times, there is so much friction between the student and the teacher that they both need a break. Most students prefer to be in their regular classes regardless of what they may say about not liking the teacher or the class.

One problem with suspending a student from a single class is the need to make sure that the student keeps up with the rest of the class. Some teachers rebel at having to prepare separate lesson assignments for a misbehaving student. There is also the problem of where to put the student during the suspension. There are only so many chairs outside of the assistant principal's office.

In-School Suspension

Some schools are fortunate enough to have special areas or classrooms for suspension programs during the school day. Students suspended from the classroom or given all-day suspensions may be placed in this special area. Some schools even send tardy students to in-school suspension. Tardy students know that if they are more than 5 minutes late to class, they must automatically go to in-school suspension. In-school suspension classes are not always staffed by certificated personnel. (See Form 10 for the In-School Suspension Assignment.)

Assignment to School Service

Assignment to school service is a growing alternative to suspension for many school districts. The key to this program's success seems to be proper supervision and parent permission.

School districts may need the approval of local district labor unions as well. Having students pick up trash, paint over graffiti, and wash restroom walls can be tricky consequences unless parents are contacted and staff is available to see that the students assigned are doing the assignment correctly.

School service does not always have to be so obviously negative. Some schools assign students to work in the library, at the reception desk, or in the cafeteria. This may seem like a reward to some adults, but the skillful administrator uses this type of assignment to build the self-concept of certain types of students.

Removal From a Class

Sometimes removal from a class is expedient for both the student and the teacher. It is usually done to prevent a more serious problem from occurring. Removal can be because of student/teacher conflict, frequent problems with other students in the class, the students are so far behind that they will never catch up, or the students are bored silly. Any of these types of conditions can result in student misbehavior. A wise school administrator takes action when these conditions are evident before a major problem occurs. It is important to consult with teachers prior to removing a student from class to help them understand why it may be necessary.

Out-of-School Suspension

Out-of-school suspension is an abused and too-often-used consequence for student misbehavior in our schools. It has become an automatic response for too many of our school administrators. Alternatives must be found so that it is not used so frequently, but there are certainly times when it is the only recourse. This is particularly true when student safety is involved. Chapter 4 will deal exclusively with suspension and expulsion procedures.

In-School Suspension Assignment

Name of School

To: _____ Date: _____

From: _____

(Name of School Administrator)

This is to inform you that _____ (name of student) has been assigned to in-school suspension for failing to abide by rules established in the Student Code of Conduct. The in-school suspension will begin on _____ and end on _____. Your assistance is necessary. Please list the assignments that will be missed during the suspension, text pages to be read, etc. _____ (name of student) will be expected to complete all work assigned by you during the period of suspension. Your assistance is sincerely appreciated and if you would like to communicate directly with the in-school suspension teacher please call my office.

Name of subject: _____

Reading assignments:

_____

_____

Review past assignments:

_____

_____

Extra assignments:

_____

_____

Special materials that should be brought to in-school suspension in addition to regular textbooks, paper, and pencil are:

_____

_____

Please place this completed form and any special workbook assignments, etc., in my box or send them to my office by 3:00 p.m. this afternoon.

Thank you for your cooperation.

_____

(Signature of School Administrator)

Assignment to a Student Court

Student courts unfortunately are a seldom-used strategy to combat student misbehavior. They can be extremely effective in reducing certain types of offenses. The rate of recidivism of misbehavior for students going before a student court is extremely low. Student courts generally follow these procedures:

- Students are referred to the student court for rule infractions related to truancy, petty theft, graffiti, or other offenses determined by the school administration to be appropriate for peer review.
- Students and their parents must agree in writing before students can go before a student court.
- Students and their parents must agree to comply with the decision of the court. If parents do not agree to have their child come before the student court, then the administrator in charge of discipline assigns the appropriate consequence.
- Student courts are conducted under the auspices of an attorney, a local magistrate, or a retired judge. In some cities, the local bar association sponsors the student court.
- Student juries hear the case and assign a consequence, if one is warranted, from a list of alternative consequences approved by the school administration.
- The jury is composed of student volunteers from a variety of classes and social groups. Care is taken not to use "pick of the litter" types of students who are involved in many school activities. A minimum of one third of the jury must be composed of students who are assigned jury duty as part of their consequence for misbehavior.
- The court generally follows the format of a traffic court for a misdemeanor offense. No witnesses are called. The offense is read by the court, and the defendants give their side of the story. The student's past record can be used by the court in making a decision.

School districts that have outstanding student court programs are Odessa, Texas, and Anchorage, Alaska. If you want to know if there are any student courts in your area, call your local bar association.

Corporal Punishment

As indicated in Chapter 1, corporal punishment is legal in 26 states of the United States. It should be noted that numerous national organizations have indicated their opposition to corporal punishment. Those organizations include the American Academy of Pediatricians, the American Counseling Association, the National Association for the Advancement of Colored People, and the National Congress of Parents and Teachers.

Administrators who use corporal punishment need to be informed of the possibility of parents' appealing to national organizations for support. In states where corporal punishment is allowed, it is generally left to the local school as to whether it should be used or not.

Corporal punishment takes many forms. In most cases, it consists of applying a paddle to the backside of the misbehaving students. Some schools use the sole of a tennis shoe, or a switch. Some schools require that the parent be present when the punishment is applied. Most schools require parent permission before corporal punishment can be applied.

Corporal punishment is sometimes used for special populations enrolled in special education classes where students seem unable to learn from normal disciplinary procedures. Obviously, there is a strict line between corporal punishment and child abuse. Schools that use corporal punishment need to be very careful not to use any type of measure that might be called abuse.

There are good reasons that many states do not allow corporal punishment. One of the chief arguments against its use is that corporal punishment can be construed to be a violent act. For many states, school districts, and school principals, corporal punishment teaches students that the use of violence to solve problems is right. It can create a high degree of anger and prove to the student that school is a negative place.

In any case, school administrators and those involved in the discipline process must be certain, prior to even considering corporal punishment as an option, to investigate whether their state or school district allows the use of corporal punishment.

CONDUCTING YOUR OWN RESEARCH ON DISCIPLINE STRATEGIES

Research is sometimes defined as taking what you think to be true and finding proof as to whether it is true or not. This is especially important when it comes to discipline. Every school administrator who is responsible for school discipline should conduct a research study at the end of the school year relating to which rule violations occurred most frequently, the types of consequences used, and the rate of student recidivism for each consequence used. Some school districts require that this be done at the end of the school year. A Discipline Year-End Summary is included as Form 11.

CONCLUSION

As indicated earlier, school discipline is a pragmatic art and not an exact science. The goal for every school administrator or other individual involved in the discipline process is to reduce the incidence of certain infractions of school rules for the coming year. The degree of self-discipline being mastered by students will be demonstrated by the number of students who need to be assigned a consequence for not following school rules.

John Dewey once said, "Discipline is the positive and constructive control over the means to achieve certain ends" (Dewey, 1913, p. 145). The ends toward which schools are working relate to academic progress and

Form 11   Discipline Year-End Summary

Discipline Year-End Summary

1. Number of referrals for violation of school rules _____

2. Number of students suspended for fighting _____
   Usual consequence assigned _____
   Number of repeat offenders _____

3. Number of students suspended for smoking _____
   Usual consequence assigned _____
   Number of repeat offenders _____

4. Number of students suspended for truancy _____
   Usual consequence assigned _____
   Number of repeat offenders _____

5. Number of students suspended for being under the
   influence of alcohol _____
   Usual consequence assigned _____
   Number of repeat offenders _____

6. Number of students suspended for suspicion of
   being under the influence of a drug _____
   Usual consequence assigned _____
   Number of repeat offenders _____

7. Number of students suspended for insubordination _____
   Usual consequence assigned _____
   Number of repeat offenders _____

8. Number of students suspended for leaving campus
   without permission _____
   Usual consequence assigned _____
   Number of repeat offenders _____

9. Number of students suspended for improper dress _____
   Usual consequence assigned _____
   Number of repeat offenders _____

10. Number of students suspended for destruction or
    defacing of school property _____
    Usual consequence assigned _____
    Number of repeat offenders _____

11. Number of students suspended for theft _____
    Usual consequence assigned _____
    Number of repeat offenders _____

12. Number of students suspended for sexual
    harassment _____

    Usual consequence assigned _____

    Number of repeat offenders _____

13. Number of students suspended for forgery
    or cheating _____

    Usual consequence assigned _____

    Number of repeat offenders _____

14. Number of students suspended for gambling _____

    Usual consequence assigned _____

    Number of repeat offenders _____

15. Number of students suspended for failure
    to attend detention or Saturday school _____

    Usual consequence assigned _____

    Number of repeat offenders _____

16. Number of students recommended for
    expulsion for sale or possession of drugs _____

    Usual consequence assigned _____

    Number of repeat offenders _____

17. Number of students recommended for
    expulsion for arson _____

    Usual consequence assigned _____

    Number of repeat offenders _____

18. Number of students recommended for
    expulsion for assault _____

    Usual consequence assigned _____

    Number of repeat offenders _____

19. Number of students recommended for
    expulsion for possession or use of a weapon _____

    Usual consequence assigned _____

    Number of repeat offenders _____

20. Other reasons for suspension or recommendations for expulsion

    _____

    _____

    _____

the ability to work with and adjust to groups. Part of the means to achieve those ends is acquired through self-discipline. Without consequences, self-discipline would be difficult to achieve. All human actions have consequences. Consequences should teach rather than punish. Punishment teaches humans to fear the environment. Consequences teach us that the results of our actions must be carefully considered prior to engaging in a specific activity. Consequences help us to develop and mature. Learning through consequences is one of the benefits of growing older. Schools that teach through consequences are helping students to mature and to reach their potential both as students and as citizens in a democratic society.

School rules are partly established by defining what the school community wants in a learning environment. Rules form a framework for achieving that end. Administrators and all those involved in the discipline process have important and powerful positions in education. Few academic disciplines or activities in schools have as much potential for student growth as the administration of discipline.

Procedural Justice and Effective School Discipline

. . . nor shall any State deprive any person of life, liberty, or property, without due process of law.

—U.S. Constitution, Amendment XIV

Procedural justice has been called "the keystone of liberty" and "the heart of the law" in our democratic society. A nation without procedural justice is subject to tyranny and the rule of a dictator. Since the Magna Carta, our legal system has relied on procedural due process as one means of ensuring fairness when a governmental agency deals with individuals. Our Bill of Rights and the Fourteenth Amendment incorporate procedural due process to guarantee freedom from arbitrary actions by federal or state government. In the words of Supreme Court Justice Felix Frankfurter: "The history of American freedom is, in no small measure, the history of procedure" (Zerle & Nalvonr, 1988, p. 67).

The National Association of Secondary School Principals (1990) *Legal Memorandum* stated:

> When the Supreme Court decided that the Constitution requires school principals and local school districts to follow procedural due process in suspension and expulsion cases, the Justices recognized an undeniable link between procedural due process and the fairness that principals know is the hallmark of effective discipline.

The Court said the Constitution requires procedural due process as a precaution "against unfair or mistaken finding of misconduct," and it described the mandated procedures as being "if anything, less than a fair-minded school principal would impose on himself to avoid unfair suspensions." (p. 1)

One of the best descriptions of the role of procedural justice in schools appears in the 1975 decision of the Supreme Court in the case of *Goss v. Lopez:*

> The authority possessed by the State to prescribe and enforce standards of conduct in its schools although concededly very broad, must be exercised consistently with constitutional safeguards. Among other things, the State is constrained to recognize a student's legitimate entitlement to a public education as a property interest that is protected by the Due Process Clause and that may not be taken away for misconduct without adherence to the minimum procedures required by that Clause.

Denying a student the right to attend school is a decision that is especially trying for any administrator who has the responsibility of controlling school environments. It is a decision that is not taken lightly. Conscientious school administrators realize that denying a property right means denying the student the opportunity to be a normal, contributing member of society. It is one of the most serious and difficult aspects of their jobs. It is a responsibility that challenges the ethical fiber of every individual who has ever had to make that decision. Every good school administrator pays close attention to due process rights as stipulated in recent decisions by the Supreme Court of the United States that relate to discipline. Most professional school administrators have had at least one course in school law. It may, however, be helpful to review "landmark cases" that have special relevance to school discipline.

LANDMARK DUE PROCESS SCHOOL DISCIPLINE CASES

Landmark cases are court cases where the rule or principle established by a court decision is so important that a groundbreaking legal principle is established. Often, landmark cases set a legal path for an institution or a group of people. For example, the case of *Brown v. the Board of Education* led the way to desegregation of schools. Six landmark cases in the area of school discipline are described.

In *In re Gault* (1966), the Supreme Court declared that "Whatever may be their precise impact, neither the Fourteenth Amendment nor the Bill of Rights is for adults alone." This ruling established that a minor in juvenile court was entitled to certain constitutional protections, including the following:

1. Knowing the charges against him or her

2. Notification of the right to counsel

3. Privilege against self-incrimination

4. Right to confrontation and cross-examination of witnesses

Although *Gault* does not apply specifically to school discipline, it is important because lower courts use the case to clarify the rights of juveniles. In *Gault,* children were stipulated as individuals who enjoy some of the same constitutional rights as adults. This case has been called a wellspring for children's rights in delinquency matters and has important implications for school discipline due process rights (*In re Gault,* 1967).

In *Tinker v. Des Moines Independent Community School District* (1969), the Supreme Court declared that the public school student comes to school protected by certain constitutional rights, and that these rights are not left "at the schoolhouse gate." This decision set the stage for much of the student rights movement of the 1970s because the decision was specifically related to the issue of free speech and the wearing of black armbands to protest the war in Vietnam. Because students are "persons" under the Constitution, school officials may constitutionally infringe on students' First Amendment rights only when the particular expression of opinion prescribed would materially and substantially interfere with the operation of the school and the rights of other students to learn (*Tinker v. Des Moines,* 1969).

In *Goss v. Lopez* (1975), the court stipulated that "a student's legitimate entitlement to a public education is a property interest that is protected by the due process clause of the Bill of Rights and forbids arbitrary deprivations of liberty." The right to attend school has been interpreted as a property right under this decision. The procedures applicable to short-term suspensions are required by the Fourteenth Amendment, which prohibits the states from impairing a person's life, liberty, or property interest without due process of law. The Court indicated that informal notice and a hearing satisfied the requirements of due process for short suspensions, and that long-term suspensions and expulsions require more formal procedures, which could include legal counsel and the right to present and confront witnesses (*Goss v. Lopez,* 1975).

In *New Jersey v. T.L.O.* (1985), the Court stated that although students are guaranteed protection against unreasonable searches and seizures without a warrant, as stipulated in the Fourth Amendment to the Constitution, there is also a "need for the maintenance of swift and informal disciplinary procedures in schools." Therefore, it may be necessary for school administrators to search students or their property without a warrant as long as the objectives of the search "are not obtrusive to the age and sex of the student and the nature of the infraction." The objectives of the search must merely be "reasonable under all circumstances" rather than the stricter "probable cause" provisions usually seen in adult cases (*New Jersey v. T.L.O.,* 1985).

The case of *New Jersey v. T.L.O.* already has broadened the administrator's right to search to be reasonable rather than held to the niceties of the probable cause standard required by police officers.

T.L.O. also set the contemporary school law trend when it indicated that schools must "strike the balance between schoolchildren's legitimate expectations of privacy and the schools' equally legitimate need to maintain an environment in which learning can take place" (*New Jersey v. T.L.O.*, 1985).

With the increase in drugs and weapons on school campuses, courts have shifted from emphasizing the individual rights of students to emphasizing the health and safety of all children who attend schools. The support of the courts for school administrators has been both helpful and encouraging.

In the case of *Doe v. Petaluma*, (1993) Jane Doe, a middle school student in Petaluma, California, was the victim of 18 months of sexually harassing remarks and behavior by her peers. Although school officials promised to end the harassment, they failed to do so; nor did they inform Jane or her parents of her rights under Title IX. The court ruled in favor of Jane Doe and established the standard that student-on-student harassment is actionable under Title IX.

In *Veronica School District v. Acton* (1995), the Supreme Court upheld as constitutional a school district policy, which required students to consent to random drug testing as a condition for participation in interscholastic athletics. The case attempted to balance a student's expectations of privacy against the government's interest in drug-free schools. The Court held that drug policy did not violate the Fourth Amendment given such factors as the athletes' relatively low expectation of privacy (e.g., due to the requirements of communal undress and preseason physical exams), the fact that the athletes were leaders in the school's drug culture, and the tests were "directed more narrowly to drug use by athletes, where the risk of immediate physical harm to the drug user or those with whom he is playing this sport is particularly high." A number of lower court decisions have qualified the implementation of the law and have attempted to test its limits: *Gardner v. Tulia Independent School District*, 2000; *Joy v. Penn-Harris-Madison School Corporation*, 2000; *Linke v. Northwestern School Corporation*, 2000; *Todd v. Rush County Schools*, 1998; *Theodore v. Delaware Valley School District*, 2003; *Trinidad School District No. 1 v. Lopez*, 1998.

LEGAL AUTHORITY FOR ADMINISTERING SCHOOLS

It is important to review the fact that school administrators receive their authority from local governing boards of education, who in turn receive their authority from both state legislatures and the electorate. The authority of school administrators will not be overturned in courts as long as two basic standards are upheld. Those two standards are described as follows:

1. Actions taken were in good faith for what is best for the school and for all those who work and attend there. Often, in the heat of dealing with a serious violation of a school rule, there is insufficient time to be certain that every legality is followed. It is important to note that school administrators are not police officers or attorneys. School administrators have the responsibility of maintaining an atmosphere in which teachers can teach and students can learn.

Although the law is not their primary responsibility, administrators must be exemplary in their efforts to be certain that the law is obeyed. In the fast-paced, pressurized world in which they work, oversights sometimes do occur. The truth is that parents cannot always be found; students do not always tell the truth; teachers, principals, and superintendents are not always available; secretaries do not always get letters finished on time; witnesses do not always volunteer information; and police officers do not always arrive promptly on the scene. Sometimes actions have to be taken swiftly to protect order and the learning environment. If a minor oversight in due process can be explained, and if the best "good faith" judgment was used considering the circumstances, there is good reason to believe that courts of law, school boards, and superintendents will be understanding.

2. There is a deliberate and wholehearted attempt to enforce state laws and district policies and rules listed in the student code of conduct. Constitutional due process requires that students be forewarned of conduct that may result in disciplinary action. For that reason, nearly every secondary school in the nation has some type of student discipline code that is issued to every student. This code is more than a simple listing of rules to follow. It has an important place in providing for due process rights of notification that belong to all citizens of the United States. Contained in that notification are certain basic fundamentals that are essential if that code is to be considered binding in a court of law.

Courts of law have indicated that the language contained in codes of conduct must be understandable, unambiguous, and clear. For example, rules proscribing "conduct inimical to the best interests of the school," prohibiting students from possessing "medicine," and banning "extreme hair styles" have been judged by the courts as being vague and therefore not to provide adequate notice (*Bertens v. Stewart*, 1984).

It is important to note that school rules can be communicated orally to students. A Texas court, for example, upheld student suspensions under a school rule that was not in writing but had been announced at several school assemblies attended by the suspended students (*New Baunfeis v. Armke*, 1983). Whether courts permit oral acceptance of school rules is up to each state legislature, but the general rule seems to be that oral rules are acceptable as long as they follow the same general outline of clarity, fairness, and unambiguous language necessary for written rules.

Student codes of conduct should include a complete explanation of the procedural rights of students in cases of suspension and expulsion. The procedures in the code should be reviewed annually by the educational staff and preferably by a committee composed of parents, students, members of the community, and even an attorney.

There are some basic checks to determine if your written rules will stand up to due process requirements:

- Watch out for *ultra vires* (beyond the school's authority) types of arguments. Does the due process action exceed the school rules and authority, and, if it does, do you have good reasons for your action (*Commonwealth v. Johnson*, 1941)? Whether or not school administrators are considered to have exceeded their authority will often depend on the reasonableness of the action.
- Are the due process portions of the rules translated into the student's native language? It may or may not be necessary, but failing to do so may leave a legal opening. Probably, most secondary school students read English, but you need to examine that assumption (Equal Educational Opportunities Act, 1974).
- Make certain you follow your own procedures. This is especially true of procedures related to suspension and expulsion (*Morton v. Ruiz*, 1974).

As long as school administrators are fulfilling their role as enforcers of rules that follow the broad framework outlined by the courts, then the actions taken are usually considered to be within the realm of good judgment and fair practice. The courts traditionally give school administrators wide latitude in fulfilling their role as administrators of order and learning in school environments.

DEVELOPING FAIR PROCEDURES FOR ALL

Goss v. Lopez (1975) has helped schools to understand that they must adhere to certain basic minimums in terms of due process rights. The "fundamental fairness" minimum that constitutional due process requires includes the following:

1. Being certain that any students who have committed a serious act of misbehavior have received notice of the charges against them and of the evidence supporting those charges

2. Being certain that any students accused of committing a serious infraction have the opportunity for a hearing at which they can defend themselves

3. Being certain that there is no delay between the time when the infraction occurred and when the student is accused and given a hearing

Most courts have been unwilling to require due process for short-term suspensions (generally five days or less), which is more complex than the informal notice and hearing described by the Supreme Court in *Goss v. Lopez.* In short-term suspensions, students may not interview witnesses or present witnesses on their behalf. Short-term suspensions are like traffic or parking citations. In short-term suspensions, the administrator in charge attempts to discover the facts and make a decision. Part of the information comes directly from the student involved in the infraction and partially from others whom the administrator may choose to interview. Students are given an opportunity to give their side of the story, a decision is made, and the students and their parents are informed of the decision and given the option of appeal. Short-term suspensions are generally simple in terms of procedural justice.

Student Searches

Due to the continuing problem of drugs on school campuses, the question of student searches has become a major procedural justice issue. In the case of *New Jersey v. T.L.O.* (1985), mentioned earlier in the chapter, the court ruled that although, in general, students are protected against unreasonable searches of their persons or their property, school officials can search students or their property as long as "it is related to the objectives of the search and not obtrusive to the age and sex of the student and the nature of the infraction." The majority opinion in the case stated the following:

> Where a careful balancing of governmental and private interests suggests that the public interest is best served by a Fourth Amendment standard of reasonableness that stops short of probable cause, we have not hesitated to adopt such a standard. . . . [B]y focusing attention on the question of reasonableness, the standard will spare teachers and school administrators the necessity of schooling themselves in the niceties of probable cause and permit them to regulate their conduct according to the dictates of reason and common sense. (*New Jersey v. T.L.O.*, 1985)

In the more recent case of *Veronica School District v. Acton* (1995), the Court further provided schools with powers necessary to combat drugs and other weapons when it allowed that although state-compelled collection of urine samples for drug-testing purposes constitutes a "search," the search in the case was reasonable because legitimate governmental interests outweighed any intrusion on a student's privacy rights. They also reasoned that when student athletes choose to go out for an athletic team, they have even less of an expectation of privacy from searches than other students. In a key statement, the Court in *Veronica* stated that public school students have a lesser expectation of privacy than members of the population generally because they are required to attend school, and because they have been committed to the temporary custody of the state as a schoolmaster. The state in its role as schoolmaster of children, may exercise a degree of supervision and control greater than it could exercise over free adults for purposes of determining reasonableness of search (*Veronica School District v. Acton*, 1995).

The effect of *Veronica* is that although school administrators must still comply with the "reasonableness" test indicated in *T.L.O.*, the parameters of the reasonableness have expanded greatly.

Lewd and Indecent Speech

Suspending students because of various expressions of opinion or speech can raise a red flag, for it may be in violation of freedom of speech provisions affirmed in the *Tinker* decision (*Tinker v. Des Moines*, 1969). In recent years, however, the Court has come down in favor of schools' inculcating the fundamental values of the community as a guideline. The case of *Bethel School District v. Fraser* (1986) emphasized that when speech is plainly offensive to both teachers and students, schools have an obligation to protect students from offensive language (*Bethel v. Fraser*, 1986). The court ruling clearly supports school officials' right to discipline students for lewd or indecent speech.

LINKING COMMUNITY SERVICES, LAW ENFORCEMENT, AND SCHOOLS FOR HIGH-RISK YOUTH

More and more states and counties are finding ways to link and communicate services rendered for high-risk youth. Chronic juvenile offenders often have school attendance problems, failure of two or more subjects, and chronic misbehavior. Early intervention with high-risk youth requires that schools communicate directly with other community and law enforcement programs in order to understand the entire environment in which the student is performing. Schools are the logical delivery site for a multidisciplinary team approach that addresses the unique educational and public safety needs of high-risk youth. California Education Code Section 47750–47751 establishes that link under law. If states do not have laws requiring such a link, then letters need to be written to state legislators requesting such a law.

CONCLUSION

To be both fair and effective, student discipline law and policy must balance two separate rights of students: the constitutional right to a public education, and the right to a safe and orderly learning environment. Laws to protect students from arbitrary and wrongful discipline are necessary, as are procedures and laws to allow schools to discipline disruptive and dangerous students. School administrators have a golden opportunity to abide by due process and to provide leadership through discipline strategies that reflect our system of procedural justice. We live in a time when school administrators must know by heart the basic elements of procedural justice that relate to school discipline. The landmark cases mentioned earlier must be part of the modern school administrator's basic vocabulary. Changes in the law reflect changes in our society, and keeping up with changes is an ongoing process. Professional organizations such as the National Association of Secondary School Administrators, the National School Safety Center, Phi Delta Kappa, and the American Bar Association make a sincere effort to keep administrators abreast of changes in the law. Keeping district administrators or county counsels current is not enough. A building administrator who is misinformed is at a serious disadvantage. Resources, including basic law books and professional periodicals, that describe changes in school law need to be available at every school. Fortunately, we live in a time of law and order, but to protect the law we need to know something about current interpretation.

Much of school law as it pertains to schools is enacted by state legislatures and is unique to individual states. This book attempts to address a national audience and does not include specific laws relative to long-term suspensions and expulsions for every state. Some general suggestions on what to include in suspension and expulsion letters are included as checklists. See Form 12 (Suspension Checklist) and Form 13 (Expulsion Checklist) at the end of Chapter 5. These checklists will provide useful guidelines that correspond to federal guidelines.

5

Suspension and Expulsion as Consequences

A student may be suspended or expelled for acts that are enumerated in state education codes or laws relating to student behavior at a school activity at any time. This includes activities while on school grounds, while going to or from school, during the lunch period while being on or off campus, during, or while going to or from a school sponsored activity. Suspension is a temporary act and expulsion may be permanent.

The preceding reasons for suspension or expulsion have been amended from time to time in most states, but overall, the reasons are generally consistent over time. Specific codes or laws related to suspension and expulsion make the school administrator's job easier and less liable. If your state does not have such a list, then every effort should be made to have the legislature adopt one. In general, suspension is used when other means of correction fail to bring about proper conduct. Most states have a limit to the number of days a student can be suspended. In most states, it cannot exceed more than 20 days in any one school year. A student cannot be suspended for more than five consecutive days at one time. Students suspended may be assigned to a supervised study area during the time of suspension providing the student poses no imminent danger to the campus, pupils, or staff, or if the action to expel the pupil has not been initiated.

During the time of suspension, the pupil is responsible for contacting his or her teacher or teachers to receive assignments to be completed while the pupil is out. Parents must be notified in writing and preferably by phone when a suspension or expulsion is assigned. It is recommended that the letter to the parents or guardians assigning suspension or expulsion be sent by registered mail and that a signature be required.

In most states, teachers can suspend a student from their class for one day and the day following the suspension. Teachers obviously must report the suspension immediately to the administrator in charge.

Students who are expelled from school may not be permitted to enroll in any other school or school district during the period of expulsion. They may attend juvenile court schools, county community schools, or other schools specifically designated by the state as schools for expelled students. The rules for each state may be different on where expelled students can go to school.

Expulsions exist for the time set forth by the governing board. The governing board may ask that students receive counseling during the time of expulsion and that the readmittance be based on requirements completed, including counseling, community service, substance abuse or other rehabilitative programs.

When a student is expelled, the pupil is entitled to a hearing to determine whether the expulsion should be upheld. In most states, the hearing must take place within 30 calendar days. The decision of the governing board to expel a pupil must be based on substantial evidence relevant to the charges adduced at the expulsion hearing. No evidence at that hearing shall be based on hearsay. A record of the hearing must be made. Sworn testimony may be used using written declarations, but they shall be examined by the hearing officer or administrative panel with the names of the persons who made the testimony. Copies without the witnesses' names must be provided to the pupil. At the request of the superintendent or the superintendent's designee, subpoenas may be used as long as they are in keeping with state law.

The final action to expel a student must be made by the governing board. In most states, only the governing board can expel a student. Parents generally have 30 days to appeal the decision of the governing board to expel to either a county or state board of education. The education code of each state would specify the regulations relating to expulsion, appeals, subpoena rights, and so on. Generally, appeals attempt to determine whether the students' rights were protected and whether the expulsion hearing was fair. It is generally the county's or state's responsibility to see that expelled students have someplace to go to school.

LONG-TERM SUSPENSION OR EXPULSION

In cases involving long-term suspension or expulsion, due process procedures are expanded. In serious cases, the student's property interest in an education is in danger. The courts have ruled that "long-term suspension and expulsion damages the student's good name and reputation, their ability to gain employment, and their opportunity to further their education" (*Cleveland Board of Education v. La Fleur,* 1974). Courts have agreed that school disciplinary procedures are not criminal proceedings, and therefore all the constitutional protections afforded to individuals accused of a crime do not apply. But the minimum requirements for due process in cases of long-term suspension or expulsion are greater than those used in simple suspensions. Following are the requirements in cases of long-term suspension or expulsion:

1. Students and their parents or guardians must be notified in writing regarding the specific charges and grounds that, if proven, would justify expulsion. The law regarding the rule or law violated should be cited.

2. Students and their parents or guardians should receive ample and timely notice of the time and place of the hearing. Notice should provide sufficient time for the accused to prepare a defense. Precisely how far in advance depends on the circumstances of the case. Some courts have held that five days should be the minimum.

3. Students and their parents or guardians should be informed of their due process rights during the hearing, which include the following:
   a. The right of students to legal counsel, who may attend the hearing along with students and their parent(s) or guardians.
   b. The right to hear and present evidence.
   c. The right to question witnesses. Students may also produce witnesses in their behalf. Different states may have different regulations concerning witnesses at expulsion hearings, particularly if they are teachers.
   d. The right to inspect student records.
   e. The right to have a record of the proceedings.
   f. The right to a speedy decision of the hearing panel, hearing officer, or governing board. Most states allow three school days.
   g. The right to appeal the decision. Students and their parents or guardians must be notified to whom the appeal can be made and the appropriate address and telephone number of the appealing person or agency.

EXCEPTIONAL CHILDREN

In the case of *Honig v. Doe* (1988), the Supreme Court ruled that school authorities may not exclude students with disabilities from school for more than 10 days without the due process provisions of the Individuals with Disabilities Educational Act (IDEA). The number of children ages 12–17 served under IDEA, Part B during the 2002–2003 school year was 2,904,282 (U.S. Department of Education, Office of Special Education Programs, July, 2003). The number of students who qualify under the law is increasing each year. The number of students who qualify as "special education" particularly in inner city schools is somewhat disturbing.

Administrators in charge of discipline sometimes feel handicapped by provisions of the law, but have learned to work within the law. The law has become so complicated and so important to the school administrator in charge of discipline that we have devoted an entire chapter, Chapter 7, to provisions of the law.

STUDENT QUESTIONING

Some educators believe that using formal questioning strategies with students smacks of police tactics. Whether or not this is the case depends to a great extent on how the questioning is conducted. But questioning is often necessary due to the increase in drugs and weapons on school campuses. As is true in society in general, procedural justice can be threatened by serious criminal activity. There is a difference between police interrogation tactics and the questioning strategies that experienced school administrators have learned over the years. Here are some questioning strategies used by experienced school administrators that do not violate student due process rights.

1. Urge the student to tell the truth, but do not threaten or "entrap" the student. Comments such as "You will feel much better if you tell me the truth" or "You will feel better if you tell the truth" are not entrapment.

2. Do not threaten or be threatening to the student. Frightened students may tell you what you want to know, but it may not be the truth. You may end up more confused than when you began.

3. Place no desks, tables, or chairs between yourself as the questioner and the student. Furniture can become a barrier to communication.

4. Place yourself between the student and the exit. The nonverbal message to students may be that if and when they tell the truth, they can leave.

5. Place yourself somewhat close to the student without violating the student's space. Be close enough to look into the student's eyes.

6. The following are possible questions to ask the student:
   a. Do you know why I am talking to you today?
   b. How do you feel about talking to me today?
   c. If you know something about this, will you tell me about it now?
   d. Are you the type of person who would do this?
   e. Tell me why you are not the one who did this?
   f. Do you know who did this?

Be certain that you do not lie, threaten, offend the student's right to be silent, physically keep the student from leaving the room, or use sarcastic or harsh language. You can usually get the truth if you are patient and thoughtful. Experienced school administrators have found that they can use questioning strategies that abide by due process and still get the job done.

EXPULSIONS

Expulsion is the most serious action that can be taken against a student. Expulsion indicates that students are not allowed to attend the schools in their local area for a specific amount of time. It takes the student away from the school community. The written language in defining acts that require expulsion is crucial. State laws usually specify the legal reasons for expelling a student from school. Although the reasons may differ slightly, there is general agreement among the states as to major reasons for expulsion. Specific state laws relating to expulsion may be found on the Web by using a search browser, the name of your state, and the words Education Code.

The language states use to identify reasons for expulsion is similar. Many follow the language of the state of California. In California, the Education Code states,

> A pupil may not be suspended from school or recommended for expulsion, unless the superintendent or the principal of the school in which the pupil is enrolled determines that the pupil has committed an act as defined pursuant to any of subdivisions (a) to (p), inclusive:
>
> (a) (1) Caused, attempted to cause, or threatened to cause physical injury to a person.
>
> (2) Willfully used force or violence upon the person of another, except in self-defense.
>
> (b) Possessed, sold, or otherwise furnished any firearm, knife, explosive, or other dangerous object . . . unless the pupil had obtained written permission to possess the item from a certificated school employee. A knife is defined as any "dirk" dagger, or other weapon with a fixed, sharpened blade fitted primarily for stabbing, a weapon with a blade longer than 3 inches, a folding knife with a blade that locks into place, or a razor with an unguarded blade.
>
> (c) Unlawfully possessed, used, sold, or otherwise furnished, or been under the influence of any controlled substance.
>
> (d) Unlawfully offered, arranged, or negotiated to sell any controlled substance listed in . . . the Health and Safety Code.
>
> (e) Committed an obscene act or engaged in habitual profanity or vulgarity.
>
> (f) Caused or attempted to cause damage to school property or private property.

(g) Possessed or used tobacco, or any products containing tobacco or nicotine on school property. No school shall permit the smoking or use of tobacco on school grounds.

(h) Stolen or attempted to steal school property or private property.

(i) Unlawfully possessed or unlawfully offered, arranged, or negotiated to sell any drug paraphernalia as defined in the Health and Safety Code.

(j) Disrupted school activities or otherwise willfully defied the valid authority of supervisors, teachers, administrators, school officials or other school personnel engaged in the performance of their duties.

(k) Knowingly received stolen school property or private property.

(l) Possessed an imitation firearm. This could be a replica so substantially similar to an existing firearm as to lead a reasonable person to conclude that the replica is a firearm.

(m) Committed or attempted to commit a sexual assault as defined in the state Penal Code.

(n) Harassed, threatened, or intimidated a pupil who is a complaining party or witness.

(o) Engaged in, or attempted to engage in, hazing.

(p) Making terrorist threats, which includes any statement, whether written or oral, which threatens to bring great bodily harm to another person or persons or property damage in excess of one thousand dollars.

ZERO TOLERANCE

In public schools, "zero tolerance" means that students are quickly suspended or expelled for violating a major school rule. Those rules are generally ones that endanger other students. Zero tolerance has been used specifically in cases of weapons or drug possession. These policies were initiated on the federal level by the 1994 Gun-Free Schools Act, which responded to several notorious school shootings across the country. The federal law required that states expel students who brought firearms to school.

Many states and school districts have gone far beyond the federal Gun-Free Schools Act by enacting policies that suspend or expel students for carrying virtually any object that could be considered a weapon, illegal drugs, prescription drugs, and even some drugs available over-the-counter. Some the most troubling stories and trends have made headlines:

- Students suspended for bringing Midol or Advil to school. (Trotter, 1996)

- Students suspended for bringing a water pistol to school. (Trotter, 1996)
- Elementary students disciplined for having plastic knives in their lunch boxes that their parents wanted them to use to cut their food. (Institute for Public Policy and Social Research, 2002)
- A student being suspended for bringing an inhaler to school. (Institute for Public Policy and Social Research, 2002)
- A kindergarten boy was suspended for having a toy knife in his possession. (Camille Jones, 2004)
- A high school junior in Philadelphia was permanently expelled from his school district for having marijuana "roaches" in his car among the garbage on the floor and a knife in the trunk. The problem was the items were in his father's car, which was parked in a church parking lot across from the high school. There was no evidence that either the marijuana or the knife belonged to the boy suspended. (Zotti, 2004)
- A high school sophomore in Topeka, Kansas, was suspended because teachers learned that he was using PHP. The principal did not know what PHP was but suspected it was a new designer drug. In reality, it is a hypertext preprocessor for a computer.

There are many examples of overly zealous administrators or school board members applying zero tolerance to ridiculous offenses. Zero tolerance is lessening in most areas of the nation while strict enforcement of school and district rules is not. Zero tolerance is much like the three strikes rule in some states. You can understand why people are concerned but the practical application makes for some very wrong conclusions. Lockstep, immediate, no-leeway rules for suspension or expulsion are bound to cause some serious errors in judgment. Although specific laws or codes related to suspension and expulsion are helpful to the school administrator, unreasonable zero tolerance laws are too strict. State laws related to suspension and expulsion should have input from experienced superintendents and principals. Knee jerk reactions applied to student behavior may be unjust and out of proportion to a minor offense. In many cases, zero tolerance is applied for political rather than discipline purposes. In other cases, it is applied out of fear and as a warning to students who might be thinking of bringing a weapon or drugs to school.

Form 12   Suspension Checklist

Suspension Checklist

Prior to suspending a student, have you done the following:

	Yes	No
Informed the student of the accusation	_____	_____
Listened to the student's side of the story	_____	_____
Located the offense in the Student Code of Conduct	_____	_____
Notified the parent or guardian	_____	_____
Talked to any witnesses, if appropriate	_____	_____

Prepared a letter to the parent that includes:

	Yes	No
• A statement of the facts leading to the decision to suspend	_____	_____
• A quotation from the law or the Student Code of Conduct relating to the rule violation	_____	_____
• A statement that indicates that the student is to remain at home under the direct supervision of the parent and is not to come to school-related activities	_____	_____
• A statement of the student's right to request a meeting with the superintendent or designee	_____	_____
• The date and time when the student will be allowed back in school	_____	_____
• A statement that indicates that the parent or guardian must accompany the student to the readmission conference	_____	_____

Form 13   Expulsion Checklist

Expulsion Checklist

Prior to recommending that a student be expelled, have you done the following:

	Yes	No
Informed the student of the accusation	_____	_____
Listened to the student's side of the story	_____	_____
Interviewed any witnesses, if appropriate	_____	_____
Informed the principal and the superintendent of the facts	_____	_____
Notified the police, if appropriate	_____	_____
Identified the legal statute, district policy, or school rule that the student has violated	_____	_____
Contacted the parent or guardian	_____	_____
Prepared the necessary information to enable the principal or the superintendent of schools to write the appropriate certified letter requiring the parent's signature, which will contain:	_____	_____

- The date and time of the hearing   _____ _____

- A statement of the facts and charges for the recommended expulsion   _____ _____

- A quotation from the state law or district policy related to the charges   _____ _____

- A notice of the student's obligation to remain at home under the direct supervision of the parent until a decision is made   _____ _____

- Notice of the opportunity for the student or the student's parent to appear in person or be represented by an attorney   _____ _____

- Notice of the parent's and student's right to inspect and obtain copies of all documents to be used at the hearing   _____ _____

- The right to confront all witnesses who testify at the hearing and the right to present oral and documentary evidence and witnesses on the student's behalf   _____ _____

Form 14   Expulsion Timeline Recommendation for States

EXPULSION TIMELINE (EC 48918)
(During summer recess, weekdays are counted as schooldays)

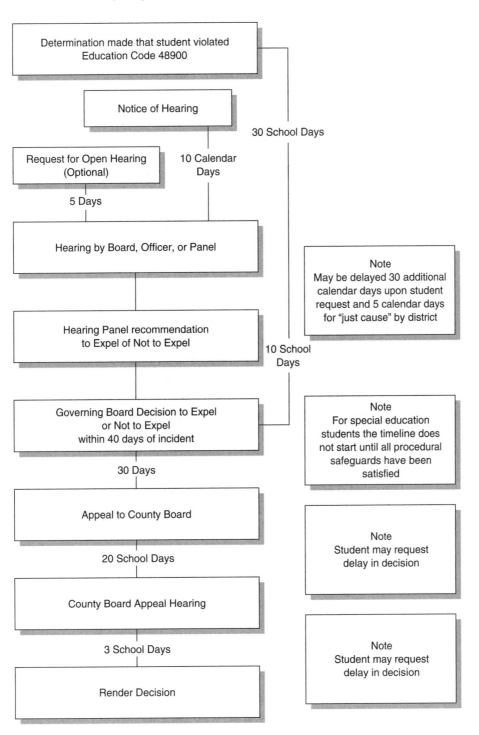

SOURCE: Used by permission from San Bernadino County, Office of Education.

6

Disciplining Students With Disabilities

In 1988, the U.S. Supreme Court held that the "stay put" provision of the Education of All Handicapped Children Act (EAHCA), now retitled the Individuals with Disabilities Educational Act (IDEA), prohibits state and local school authorities from unilaterally excluding children from the classrooms and schools for dangerous or disruptive conduct growing out of their disabilities. In the case of *Honig v. Doe*, the court ruled that school authorities may not exclude students with disabilities from school for more than 10 days without the due process procedures of the EAHCA. The court also ruled that school authorities may use procedures (including a suspension for up to 10 school days) to deal with students who pose an immediate danger to themselves or others, or who cause substantial disruption of classrooms or the school as cited in earlier cases (*Honig v. Doe*, 1988).

There is a disagreement as to whether a school district must continue to provide services for students with disabilities after they are expelled. The U.S. Office of Special Education and Rehabilitative Services (OSERS) says it is necessary, but the U.S. Ninth Circuit Court of Appeals disagrees, saying that if the behavior is not a part of the child's disability, then the district has no responsibility to provide additional services (*Doe v. Maher*, 1986). It is important to note that if school districts are going to expel a student with a disability, then they must make careful notes as to what efforts they have made to instruct the student in appropriate behavior while on the school grounds. Working with teachers and classroom aides is crucial to establish that instruction has occurred.

INDIVIDUALS WITH DISABILITIES EDUCATION ACT

The Individuals with Disabilities Education Act (IDEA; formerly called P.L. 94–142 or the Education for All Handicapped Children Act of 1975) requires public schools to make available to all eligible children with disabilities a free appropriate public education in the least restrictive environment appropriate to their individual needs.

IDEA requires public school systems to develop appropriate Individualized Education Programs (IEPs) for each child. The specific special education and related services outlined in each IEP reflect the individualized needs of each student.

IDEA also mandates that particular procedures be followed in the development of the IEP. Each student's IEP must be developed by a team of knowledgeable persons and must be at least reviewed annually. The team includes the child's teacher; the parents, subject to certain limited exceptions; the child, if determined appropriate; an agency representative who is qualified to provide or supervise the provision of special education; and other individuals at the parents' or agency's discretion.

If parents disagree with the proposed IEP, they can request a due process hearing and a review from the state educational agency if applicable in that state. They also can appeal the state agency's decision to state or federal court.

Prior to the amendments to the EAHCA in 1975, the special educational needs of children with disabilities were not being met. More than half of the children with disabilities in the United States did not receive appropriate educational services, and a million children with disabilities were excluded entirely from the public school system. All too often, school officials used disciplinary measures to exclude children with disabilities from education simply because they were different or more difficult to educate than nondisabled children.

It is against that backdrop that Pub. L. 94–142 was developed, with one of its primary goals being the elimination of any exclusion of children with disabilities from education. In the IDEA preauthorization of 1997, Congress recognized that flexibility in the administration of the Act was necessary, and certain sections of the Act were used to justify exclusion and what constitutes a change in placement.

Recent Changes in IDEA

Some of the recent changes in IDEA reflect the concerns of school administrators and teachers regarding preserving school safety and order, while helping schools respond appropriately to a child's behavior, promoting the use of appropriate behavioral interventions, and increasing the likelihood of success in school and school completion for some of our most at-risk students. The following is a summary of recent changes quoted from the U.S. Department of Education, Office of Special Education Programs, Office of Special Education and Rehabilitative Services:

Limitations in the statute and regulations about the amount of time that a child can be removed from his or her current placement only come into play when schools are not able to work out an appropriate placement with the parents of a child who has violated a school code of conduct. In many, many cases involving discipline for children with disabilities, schools and parents are able to reach an agreement about how to respond to the child's behavior. In addition, neither the statute nor the proposed or final regulations impose absolute limits on the number of days that a child can be removed from his or her current placement in a school year.

School personnel have the ability to remove a child for short periods of time as long as the removal does not constitute a change of placement. To help make this point, the regulations include a new provision (Section 300.519) that reflects the department's long-standing definition of what constitutes a "change of placement" in the disciplinary context. In this regulation, a disciplinary "change of placement" occurs when a child is removed for more than 10 consecutive school days or when the child is subjected to a series of removals that constitute a pattern because they cumulate to more than 10 school days in a school year, *and* because of factors such as the length of the removal, the total amount of time the child is removed, and the proximity of the removals to one another. (Section 300.519). Changes also have been made to Section 300.520(a)(1) to make clear that multiple short-term removals (i.e., 10 consecutive days or less) for separate incidents of misconduct are permitted, to the extent removals would be applied to children without disabilities as long as those removals do not constitute a change of placement, as defined in Section 300.519.

Instead of requiring that services begin on the eleventh day in a school year that a child is removed from his or her current educational placement, the regulations take a more flexible approach. If the removal is pursuant to school personnel's authority to remove for not more than 10 consecutive days or for behavior that is not a manifestation of the child's disability, consistent with services must be provided to the extent necessary to enable the child to continue to appropriately progress in the general curriculum and appropriately advance toward the goals in his or her IEP (Section 300.121(d)).

If the removal is by school personnel under their authority to remove for not more than 10 school days at a time, school personnel, in consultation with the child's special education teacher, make the determination regarding the extent to which services are necessary to meet this standard.

If the removal constitutes a change in placement, the child's IEP team must be involved. If the removal is pursuant to the authority to discipline a child with a disability to the same extent as a nondisabled child for behavior that has been determined to not be a manifestation of the child's disability (Section 300.524), the child's IEP team makes the determination regarding the extent to which services are necessary to meet this standard. If the child is being placed in an interim alternative educational setting for up to 45 days because of certain weapon or drug offenses or because a hearing officer has determined that there is a substantial likelihood of injury to the child or others if the child remains in his or her current placement, the services to be provided to the child are determined based on Section 300.522 of the law. In these cases, the interim alternative educational setting must be selected so as to enable the child to continue to progress in the general curriculum, although in another setting, and to continue to receive those services and modifications, including those described in the child's current IEP, that will enable the child to meet the goals set out in that IEP and include services and modifications to address the behavior.

Under these regulations, IEP team meetings regarding functional behavioral assessments and behavioral intervention plans will only be required within 10 business days of when the child is first removed for more than 10 school days in a school year, and whenever the child is subjected to a disciplinary change of placement (Section 300.520(b)(1)). In other subsequent removals in a school year when a child already has a functional behavioral assessment and behavioral intervention plan, the IEP team members can review the behavioral intervention plan and its implementation in light of the child's behavior, without a meeting, and only meet if one or more of the team members believe that the plan or its implementation needs modification (Section 300.520).

These final regulations also provide that manifestation determinations, and the IEP team meetings to make these determinations, are only required when a child is subjected to a disciplinary change of placement (Section 300.523(a)). These changes should eliminate the need for unnecessary, repetitive IEP team meetings. (U.S. Department of Education, 2004)

WHY ARE THERE SPECIAL RULES ABOUT DISCIPLINE FOR CHILDREN WITH DISABILITIES?

The protections in the IDEA regarding discipline are designed to prevent the type of often speculative and subjective decision making by school officials that led to widespread abuses of the rights of children with disabilities to an appropriate education in the past. For example, in *Mills v. Board of Education of the District of Columbia* (1972) the court recognized that many children were being excluded entirely from education merely because they had been identified as having a behavior disorder. It is important to keep in mind, however, that these protections do not prevent school officials from maintaining a learning environment that is safe and conducive to learning for all children. Well run schools that have good leadership, well-trained teachers, and high standards for all students have fewer discipline problems than schools that do not.

It is also extremely important to keep in mind that the provisions of the statute and regulation concerning the amount of time a child with a disability can be removed from regular placement for disciplinary reasons are only called into play if the removal constitutes a change of placement, and the parent objects to proposed action by school officials (or objects to a refusal by school officials to take an action) and requests a due process hearing. The discipline rules concerning the amount of time a child can be removed from current placement essentially are exceptions to the generally applicable requirement that a child remains in current placement during the pendency of due process, and subsequent judicial, proceedings. (See Section 615(j) of the Act and Section 300.514.)

If school officials believe that a child's placement is inappropriate, they can work with the child's parents through the IEP and placement processes to come up with an appropriate placement for the child that will meet the needs of the child and result in improved learning for that child and others and ensure a safe environment. In addition to the other measures discussed in the following questions, the discipline provisions of the IDEA allow responsible and appropriate changes in placement of children with disabilities when their parents do not object.

DOES IDEA CONTAIN PROVISIONS THAT PROMOTE PROACTIVE UP-FRONT MEASURES THAT WILL HELP PREVENT DISCIPLINE PROBLEMS?

1. Research has shown that if teachers and other school personnel have the knowledge and expertise to provide appropriate behavioral interventions, future behavior problems can be greatly diminished if not totally avoided. Appropriate staff development activities and improved preservice training programs at the university level with emphasis in the area of early identification of reading and behavior problems and appropriate interventions can help to ensure that regular and special education teachers and other school personnel have the needed knowledge and skills. Changes in the IDEA emphasize the need of state and local educational agencies to work to ensure that superintendents, principals, teachers, and other school personnel are equipped with the knowledge and skills that will enable them to appropriately address behavior problems when they occur.

2. In addition, the IDEA includes provisions that focus on individual children. If a child has behavior problems that interfere with the child's learning or the learning of others, the IEP team must consider whether strategies, including positive behavioral interventions, strategies, and supports, are needed to address the behavior. If the IEP team determines that such services are needed, they must be added to the IEP and must be provided. The U.S. Department of Education has supported a number of activities such as training institutes, conferences, clearinghouses, and other technical assistance and research activities on this topic to help school personnel appropriately address behavioral concerns for children with disabilities.

CAN A CHILD WITH A DISABILITY WHO IS EXPERIENCING SIGNIFICANT DISCIPLINARY PROBLEMS BE REMOVED TO ANOTHER PLACEMENT?

Yes. Even when school personnel are appropriately trained and are probatively addressing children's behavior issues through positive behavioral intervention supports, interventions, and strategies, there may be instances when a child must be removed from current placement. When there is agreement between school personnel and the child's parents regarding a change in placement (as there frequently is), there will be no need to bring into play the discipline provisions of the law. Even if agreement is not possible, in general, school officials can remove any child with a disability from regular school placement for up to 10 school days at a time, even over the parents' objections, whenever discipline is appropriate and is administered consistent with the treatment of nondisabled children (Section 300.520(a)(1)). However, school officials cannot use this authority to repeatedly remove a child from current placement if that series of removals means the child is removed for more than 10 school days in a school year and factors such as the length of each removal, the total amount of time that the child is removed, and the proximity of the removals to one another lead to the conclusion that there has been a change in placement (Sections 300.519–300.520(a)(1)). There is no specific limit on the number of days in a school year that a child with a disability can be removed from current placement. After a child is removed from current placement for more than 10 cumulative school days in a school year, services must be provided to the extent required under Section 300.121(d) for children suspended or expelled from school.

If the child's parents do not agree to a change of placement, school authorities can unilaterally remove a child with a disability from the child's regular placement for up to 45 days at a time if the child has brought a weapon to school or to a school function, or knowingly possessed or used illegal drugs, or sold or solicited the sale of controlled substances while at school or a school function (Section 300.520(a)(2)).

In addition, if school officials believe that a child with a disability is substantially likely to injure self or others in the child's regular placement, they can ask an impartial hearing officer to order that the child be removed to an interim alternative educational setting for a period of up to 45 days (Section 300.521). If at the end of an interim alternative educational placement of up to 45 days, school officials believe that it would be dangerous to return the child to the regular placement because the child would be substantially likely to injure self or others in that placement, they can ask an impartial hearing officer to order that the child remain in an interim alternative educational setting for an additional 45 days (Section 300.526(c)). If necessary, school officials can also request subsequent extensions of these interim alternative educational settings for up to 45 days at a time if school officials continue to believe that the child would be substantially likely to injure self or others if returned to regular placement (Section 300.526(c)(4)). Additionally, at any time, school officials may seek to obtain a court order to remove a child with a disability from school or to change a child's current educational placement if they believe that maintaining the child in the current educational placement is substantially likely to result in injury to the child or others. Finally, school officials can report crimes committed by children with disabilities to appropriate law enforcement authorities to the same extent as they do for crimes committed by nondisabled students (Section 300.529).

CAN A CHILD WITH A DISABILITY BE REMOVED FROM PLACEMENT FOR MORE THAN TEN DAYS IN A SCHOOL YEAR?

No. School authorities may unilaterally suspend a child with a disability from the child's regular placement for not more than 10 school days at a time for any violation of school rules if nondisabled children would be subjected to removal for the same offense. They also may implement additional suspensions of up to 10 school days at a time in that same school year for separate incidents of misconduct if educational services are provided for the remainder of the removals, to the extent required under Section 300.121(d). (See the next question regarding the provision of educational services during periods of removal.) However, school authorities may not remove a child in a series of short-term suspensions (up to 10 school days at a time) if these suspensions constitute a pattern that is a change of placement because the removals cumulate to more than 10 school days in a school year and because of factors such as the length of each removal, the total amount of time the child is removed, and the proximity of the removals to one another. But not all series of removals that cumulate to more than 10 school days in a school year would constitute a pattern under Section 300.519(b).

Of course, in the case of less serious infractions, schools can address the misconduct through appropriate instructional and related services, including conflict management, behavior management strategies, and measures such as study carrels, time-outs, and restrictions in privileges, so long as they are not inconsistent with the child's IEP. If a child's IEP or behavior intervention plan addresses a particular behavior, it generally would be inappropriate to utilize some other response, such as suspension, to that behavior.

AFTER THE TENTH SCHOOL DAY THEN WHAT?

Beginning on the eleventh cumulative day in a school year that a child with a disability is removed from current placement, the school district must provide those services that school personnel (for example, the school administrator or other appropriate school personnel) in consultation with the child's special education teacher determine to be necessary to enable the child to appropriately progress in the general curriculum and appropriately advance toward achieving the goals set out in the child's IEP. School personnel would determine where those services would be provided. This means that for the remainder of the removal that includes the eleventh day, and for any subsequent removals, services must be provided to the extent determined necessary, while the removal continues (Section 300.121(d)(2) and (3)).

Not later than 10 business days after removing a child with a disability for more than 10 school days in a school year, the school district must convene an IEP team meeting to develop a behavioral assessment plan if the district has not already conducted a functional behavioral assessment and implemented a behavioral intervention plan for the child. If a child with a disability who is being removed for the eleventh cumulative school day in a school year already has a behavioral intervention plan, the school district must convene the IEP team (either before or not later than 10 business days after first removing the child for more than 10 school days in a school year) to review the plan and its implementation, and modify the plan and its implementation as necessary to address the behavior (Section 300.520(b)).

A manifestation determination would not be required unless the removal that includes the eleventh cumulative school day of removal in a school year is a change of placement (Section 300.523(a)).

EXPULSION OF STUDENTS WITH DISABILITIES

Does the IDEA or its regulations mean that children with disabilities can never be suspended for more than 10 school days at a time or expelled for behavior that is not a manifestation of their disabilities? No. If the IEP team concludes that the child's behavior was not a manifestation of the child's disability, the child can be disciplined in the same manner as nondisabled children, except that appropriate educational services must be provided (Section 300.524(a)). This means that if nondisabled children are long-term suspended or expelled for a particular violation of school rules, the child with disabilities may also be long-term suspended or expelled. Educational services must be provided to the extent the child's IEP team determines necessary to enable the child to appropriately progress in the general curriculum and appropriately advance toward the goals set out in the child's IEP (Section 300.121(d)(2)).

WEAPONS POSSESSION BY STUDENTS WITH DISABILITIES

Does the statutory language "carries a weapon to school or to a school function" cover instances in which the child acquires a weapon at school? Yes. Although the statutory language "carries a weapon to school or to a school function" could be viewed as ambiguous on this point, in light of the clear intent of Congress in the Act to expand the authority of school personnel to immediately address school weapons offenses, the U.S. Department of Education's opinion is that this language also covers instances in which the child is found to have a weapon obtained while at school.

NOTE: For the full text of specific information about federal regulations related to IDEA contact:

Office of Special Education Programs
Office of Special Education and Rehabilitative Services
U.S. Department of Education
400 Maryland Avenue, S.W.
Washington, D.C. 20202-7100
www.ed.gov/about/offices/list/osers/osep/index.html?svc=mr

7

Best Strategies to Keep Your School Safe

School safety has rightfully been an area of emphasis for school administrators over the past 10 years. Very large and important research studies have been completed in recent years that provide a research base for policies and measures school administrators should pay attention to in order to make their schools a safe place where teachers can teach and students can learn. It is important to emphasize, when discussing safe schools strategies, that nearly every recent study of schools on a national basis indicates that serious violent crime on school campuses is rare. However, schools have experienced high levels of less serious violent crime and property crime that has compromised instruction in many classrooms. This is particularly true in middle schools. A study by Gottfredson Associates for the U.S. Department of Education in 2002 of 886 elementary and secondary principals indicated that 66% of their schools experienced one or more incidents of less serious crime (i.e., fighting without a weapon, vandalism, or theft), and 10% experienced at least one serious violent crime (fighting with a weapon or robbery). Compared with elementary and high schools, middle schools had higher levels of many types of problem behavior. According to principal reports, 21% of middle schools had one or more incidents of physical attack or fight with a weapon, compared to 2% of elementary schools and 11% of high schools. Principals also reported that 72% of middle schools experienced fights without a weapon, compared to 34% of elementary schools and 56% of high schools. There are many excellent studies available of violence prevention. There is such a great amount of research that it is difficult for busy school administrators to know which studies to read and which to follow. Many studies are available online and can be obtained free of charge. The following is a list of six of the best national studies and where they can be obtained:

1. *Threat Assessment in Schools: A Guide to Managing Threatening Situations and Creating Safe School Climates* (Fein et al., 2002).
   www.secretservice.gov/ntac.shtml
   www.ed.gov/pubs/edpubs.html
   1-877-4-ED-PUBS

2. *Wide Scope, Questionable Quality: Drug and Violence Prevention Efforts in American Schools. Report on the Study on School Violence and Prevention* (Crosse et al., 2001).
   www.edpubs.org
   1-877-4-ED-PUBS

3. *A Closer Look at Drug and Violence Prevention Efforts in American Schools: Report on the Study on School Violence and Prevention* (Cantor et al., 2001).
   www.edpubs.org
   1-877-4-ED-PUBS

4. *School Crime Patterns: A National Profile of U.S. Public High Schools Using Rates of Crime Reported to Police. Report of the Study of School Violence and Prevention* (Cantor et al., 2001).
   www.edpubs.org
   1-877-4-ED-PUBS

5. *Early Warning, Timely Response: A Guide to Safe Schools* (Dwyer et al., 1998).
   www.ed.gov/about/offices/list/osers/osep/gtss.html

6. *Exemplary and Promising Safe, Disciplined, and Drug-Free Schools Programs* (U.S. Department of Education, 2001).
   www.edpubs.org
   1-877-4-ED-PUBS

These studies represent years of research using data from thousands of schools throughout the United States. The researchers are highly qualified researchers and practitioners, and their findings need to be carefully regarded by school personnel. Because the research is so extensive, it is not possible to summarize the reports in any effective manner. It is possible to underline some important facts that point administrators in the right direction while they find time to read the research studies. It is recommended that administrators send for the studies and keep them on their bookshelf.

One of the most recent studies, the U.S. Department of Education, National Center for Statistics, *School Survey on Crime and Safety* (2000), reveals some important facts about violence and crime in schools. The survey was a nationally representative sample of 2,270 regular public elementary, middle, secondary, and combined schools in the United States.

- In 1999–2000, 71% of public elementary and secondary schools experienced at least one violent incident. Approximately 1.5 million incidents of theft and violence occurred in about 59,000 public schools that year.
- In the same year, 20% of public schools experienced at least one incident that could be called "serious" (including rape, sexual battery other than rape, physical attacks or fights with a weapon, threats of physical attack with a weapon, and robberies either with or without a weapon).
- Schools were more likely to have experienced at least one physical attack or fight without a weapon than any other type of crime (64%). Threats of physical attack without a weapon (52%) and vandalism (51%) were the second most reported crimes during 1999–2000, followed by theft or larceny (46%) and possession of a knife or sharp object (43%).
- Sexual battery other than rape (2%), rape or attempted rape (1%), and robbery with a weapon (0%) were least likely to occur at school.
- Discipline statistics in the studies are also interesting. Some highlights include
  - Schools reported bullying (29%) as the serious discipline problem that occurred most frequently.
  - Student acts of disrespect for teachers was reported as the second most frequent serious discipline problem by 19% of schools.
  - Nineteen percent reported undesirable gang activities as a serious discipline problem.
  - Serious disciplinary action was taken by 54% of the public schools for offenses listed as "serious." There were 1,163,000 actions. Of those serious disciplinary actions, 83% were suspensions, 11% were expulsions, and 7% were transfers to specialized schools. Included in those actions were the following serious disciplinary actions and their percentages:
    - Use of a firearm or explosive device, 2%
    - Possession of a firearm or explosive device, 4%
    - Use of a weapon other than a firearm or explosive device, 5%
    - Possession of a weapon other than a firearm, 19%
    - Distribution of illegal drugs, 10%
    - Possession or use of illegal drugs or alcohol, 20%
    - Fights, 35%
    - Threats, 22%
    - Insubordination, 18%

Other important and interesting statistics for a school administrator include the following:

- A 2003 National Youth Gang Survey indicated that 38% of suburban counties and 12% of rural counties reported gang activities (Office of Juvenile Justice and Delinquency Prevention, 1999).
- There has been a 50% increase in gang killings since 1999 (Office of Juvenile Justice and Delinquency Prevention, 1999).
- The number of street gangs in the United States has doubled since 1995 (Office of Juvenile Justice and Delinquency Prevention, 1999).
- An estimated 42% of youth gangs in the United States were involved in the street sale of drugs between 1996 and 1997 (Office of Juvenile Justice and Delinquency Prevention, 1999).
- Middle schools experience more problem behavior than other schools. During the 1997–1998 school year, 21% of middle schools had one or more incidents of physical attack or a fight with a weapon compared to 2% of elementary schools and 11% of high schools (Crosse et al., 2001).
- Nineteen percent of middle school students were physically attacked in school compared with 10% of high school students (Cross et al., 2001).
- Eight percent of middle school students were robbed of $1 or more in school, compared with 4% of high school students (Cross et al., 2001).

Despite these rather alarming statistics, all of the six research studies mentioned above indicate that schools are relatively safe places and are nearly always safer than the communities in which they are located. Although the national crime rates are down, serious discipline cases in schools do not reflect that decline. Schools reflect the communities in which they are located, but in many cases, crime rates and serious school discipline offenses are not parallel. This is particularly true in our nation's middle schools. There are still over 200 million guns in the United States, and the availability of weapons remains a serious and long-standing threat to children and youth.

With all the emphasis on curriculum improvements and "raising the bar of expectations of student achievement" (No Child Left Behind Act, 2002), it is necessary for principals to pay attention to continuously improving school discipline procedures and practices. Without good discipline practices and safe schools, curriculum innovation, higher standards, and good teaching may not be possible. Good discipline practices must not be an afterthought of higher standards. Good discipline must be the mainstay and starting point of good schools.

The six studies mentioned earlier do have some common threads in terms of what school administrators can do in relation to keeping their schools safe from violence and drugs. They can be divided into three categories organized along the common threads: prevention, discovery, and remedies.

1. **Prevention.** What can schools do to prevent students from using harmful drugs or possessing weapons on school campuses?

2. **Discovery.** What can schools do to improve their efforts to find drugs and weapons on school campuses?

3. **Remedies.** What can be done with students found guilty of selling, buying, or possessing drugs or weapons on school campuses?

PREVENTION STRATEGIES

A good prevention program focuses on factual information and instruction. Students need to know why they should not take drugs or bring weapons to school. They need to have some accurate information about the effects of drugs and the risks they take if they carry a weapon.

Instruction should not be moralistic or pedantic. Today's students are bright and sophisticated. If the facts are presented to them in a straightforward and honest fashion, we have a better chance of influencing their behavior. The use of experts can be helpful providing they are good communicators with youth and use materials that do not patronize students. The entire school staff should discuss ways to best present prevention information.

Keeping Unwanted Strangers off Your School Campus

An informal survey of more than 100 school administrators indicated that approximately half the drug sales and half the violence that occurred on their school campuses were initiated by visitors to the campus. Keeping unwanted visitors off your school campus is expensive because it requires additional campus proctors and, in some areas, campus security personnel. It also requires a close link between the school administrative staff and local law enforcement agencies. Ways to keep unwanted adults off your school campus include the following:

- Establish a campus **intruder and visitor screening** procedure. All visitors to the school should be issued a badge to be worn while on the school grounds.
- Post **All visitors must report to the office** signs near every entrance to the campus.
- Use well-trained and experienced **campus proctors** who have quality walkie-talkies at their disposal so they may report intruders from a distance.
- Ask for assistance from **local law enforcement** agencies. Law enforcement officers often know who the undesirables are in any community and whether they belong on or near a school campus.
- Ask **student leaders** to help spot nonstudents. Student leaders generally want to keep their schools free of drugs and weapons.
- Keep **student and faculty parking lots** closed. Parking lots can be inviting places for off-campus visitors.
- Ask your local law enforcement agency to park **patrol cars in front of the school** at the beginning and the end of the school day. Their

presence alone will be a deterrent to off-campus visitors. If your athletic fields are open, you may want to ask the local law enforcement agency to park a patrol car near the athletic fields as well. Athletic fields are frequently used places to transfer drugs or weapons because the open areas allow one to see police or school supervisors from a distance.

- Ask for persons who live near the school to be a part of your local **neighborhood watch program.** Neighbors should be encouraged to report unknown adult persons loitering in alleys or passageways near the school as well as near their homes.
- Do not allow strangers to attend school dances without a school administrator's **interviewing the individual in advance.**
- **Post signs** that indicate that persons who do not belong on or near the school campus will be prosecuted. The sign should cite the appropriate city anti-loitering or other state laws relating to trespassing on a school campus.

Make certain every student has a **photo ID** and that the office has a copy of the student's photo as well. Identification of your own students in large schools may be a problem. The police and campus proctors may need to use IDs because they do not know who is a student and who is not. Notify students that they should have the identification card with them at all times.

Break the "Code of Silence" on Your Campus

In many schools, there is a pervasive sense among students and some adults that telling grownups that another student is posing a threat or planning a dangerous act is breaking an unwritten "code of silence." This type of "code" is dangerous to the school, its students, and teachers. Studies indicate that most shooters shared their lethal plans with other students, but those students rarely told adults.

In a climate of safety, students are willing to break the code of silence. The need to break that code is of paramount importance for a truly safe school. The U.S. Secret Service and U.S. Department of Education Guide, *Threat Assessment in Schools* (Fein et al., 2002) makes the following recommendations to break the code of silence.

1. **Assess the school's emotional climate**. Take a "step back" and gain perspective on your school from the student's point of view (see Chapter 7). Give a survey on the degree of fairness on your school campus (see Chapter 1) to a sampling of students. Is your campus free of threats from insiders as well as outsiders? Is there a degree of trust between students, teachers, and administrators?

2. **Emphasize the importance of listening**. Do teachers and administrators really listen to students, and do the students listen to adults? Listening is a "two way street." Listening is especially important when it comes to feelings.

3. **Take a strong stand against the code of silence**. Ask a group of art students to prepare some clever posters with clever sayings that perhaps members of your student council prepared (e.g., Real friends dare to tell when danger is around).

Using School Success Stories

Another prevention strategy that can be effective is publicizing the increase in the number of students going on to college, the decrease in the dropout rate, improved test scores, and individual student success stories. This type of factual information should be part of your drugs and weapons prevention plan. Students should know that succeeding in school is the norm, and that those who take drugs or carry weapons are not in the mainstream. How you are perceived by others is crucial to the self-concept of every adolescent. Ways must be found to portray those who engage in drugs and weapons as losers who should be pitied and not emulated. Using posters of national figures who have died from a drug overdose or from violence has been found to be an effective prevention strategy.

Citing the Legal Consequences

Teachers and administrators need to remind students that possessing drugs or weapons on a school campus is a serious crime. If they are found with either drugs or weapons, they are subject to criminal prosecution as well as possible expulsion from the school district. There is no argument about whether the weapon or the drug was dangerous. Possession of illegal drugs or weapons is against the law.

Students will be prosecuted under the fullest extent of the law and will lose their right to attend school. This must be made clear. There is zero tolerance for drugs or weapons in schools, and student offenders will be caught and punished. Research indicates that certainty of punishment is an effective deterrent to crime.

Explaining the Physical Dangers

Teachers can help by explaining the physical dangers related to alcohol, marijuana, heroin, crack cocaine, and possessing a weapon in their classroom presentations. Substance abuse and weapons prevention must be a part of the total school curriculum if prevention is to be effective. Experimenting with drugs or showing off with a weapon is dangerous, and students cannot be told the facts too often. Teachers should help students understand the following facts:

- During the teen years, the central nervous system is still developing, and using drugs may impair normal development and cause permanent brain damage.
- Psychoactive drugs affect your brain and impair judgment. Under their influence, you are more likely to endanger your life or the life

of a friend. You are also less able to protect yourself from physical or sexual assault.

- Drugs are addictive. You are not in control of how they affect you. You can become dependent on them very quickly.
- Marijuana is illegal and a possible gateway to more dangerous drugs.
- Alcohol-related driving accidents, violence, and suicide are the three main causes of death for teenagers.
- Cigarette smoking can be a gateway to drugs. Teenagers who smoke are 5.9 times more likely to use illegal drugs (Columbia University Center for Alcohol and Substance Abuse, 1994).
- Gunshot wounds are the leading cause of death for both black and white teenage boys in America (American Medical Association, 1992).
- Using a weapon against someone else is likely to provoke revenge in others, which may result in violence against you.
- Guns are not toys. The purpose of a bullet is to maim and kill.
- Striking someone with an object can destroy that person's life forever. You may pay the consequences for destroying someone else's life the rest of your life.

Other Prevention Strategies

Posters

Making facts into posters can be helpful. You can request posters and other information from the U.S. Department of Education, Drug Planning and Outreach Program, 400 Maryland Ave., SW, Room 4145, Washington, DC 20202, or the Center for the Control of Handgun Violence, 1225 I Street, NW, Suite 1100, Washington, DC 20005.

Curricula

There are many substance abuse and violence prevention curricula available on the market. Most school districts have a staff person who specializes in substance abuse prevention curricula. To request a list of available substance abuse prevention curricula, write to the National Clearinghouse for Alcohol and Drug Information, PO Box 2345, Rockville, MD 29852.

School Assemblies

Having a school assembly at least once a year that deals with the dangers of drugs and violence can be helpful. Resource speakers are available from your local bar association, medical society, police department, or U.S. Department of Justice. Having a film by itself may not be effective. A guest speaker, with a film or slides followed by classroom discussion, is the best and most effective scenario.

DISCOVERY STRATEGIES

Ways need to be found to discover those students who are using or selling drugs or bringing weapons onto the school campus. Discovery strategies have received a great deal of attention in recent years. But discovery by itself is not the answer to drugs or weapons on school campuses. The fact that you catch a few students may not mean that you have decreased the problem. Unfortunately, drug availability has remained largely unchanged over the last several years. A recent study by the Centers for Disease Control and Prevention (2003) indicated that 27.8% of students asked indicated that they had been offered, sold, or given an illegal drug on school property in the last 12 months. Discovery is only one segment of what should be a three-pronged approach of prevention, discovery, and remedies. Often-used discovery strategies for drugs and weapons include the following:

- **Locker searches,** usually conducted on a random basis.
- **Drug-sniffing dogs,** generally used on a random basis.
- **Metal detectors,** generally used on a random basis.
- **Urine testing** of athletes, usually conducted on a random basis.
- **Undercover police officers** posing as students, making drug buys.
- Search of suspected students, **book bags, purses, or pockets.**
- Searching **bushes and areas on the perimeter** of the school where drugs or weapons could be stashed on days when drug or weapons searches are held.

It is important to remember that *New Jersey v. T.L.O.* (1985) indicated that school administrators need only "reasonable cause" to search a student, which is a far looser restriction than "probable cause." *Veronica School District v. Acton* (1995) demonstrated that urine testing for athletes was legal, but the reasonableness and privacy rules still apply. It is also important to note that strip searches and other gross violations of individual liberty are not appropriate discovery techniques. Care must also be taken to not concentrate your search efforts on one race or ethnic group.

Conducting Random Metal Detector Searches

Most schools conduct some type of mass search strategy during the school year. Metal detectors can be used in all these searches. Metal detector searches have the advantage of demonstrating to the students that the administration is serious about preventing drugs and violence. Metal detector searches may be an effective deterrent even if no weapons are found. Metal detectors are available from a number of sources. Your local airport security office will tell you the best local source of a metal detector.

The Los Angeles Unified School District uses the following procedure when it conducts a metal detector search:

    I. Determine the location and the time when the search is to occur.

   II. The scan team sets up the scan area.

  III. The selection teams go and pick up students, selected on a random basis.

  IV. Students enter the scan area.
      A. Students are advised why they are in the room.
      B. Scanning and searches take place.
         1. Advise students to take their coats off and place their belongings on the table. Also advise students to take anything made of metal out of their pockets and place them on the tray.
         2. Advise students that those who refuse to cooperate will be referred to the principal or another designee.
         3. The weapon-scanning person will proceed in the following manner:
            • Stand to the left side of the individual to be scanned.
            • Move to the rear of the subject and scan the left side from the feet to the head.
            • Scan the back of the subject from the head to the feet.
            • Scan the subject's right side from the head to the feet.
            • Scan frontal areas of the student from head to foot.

If the person conducting the search notices an object that may activate the metal-detecting device, the person should ask the individual to remove the object or should remove the object from the individual. If the individual refuses or a more detailed search is needed, the scanner should contact a school administrator or a campus security officer.

A diagram showing the proper scanning procedure is provided in Figure 7.1.

REMEDIES, CONSEQUENCES, AND DETERRENTS AS STRATEGIES

The term *remedy* is often used interchangeably with the terms *consequence* or *punishment* when applied to school discipline practices. Remedies for drug or weapon possession generally involve recommendations for expulsion from the school district. Remedies for drug use may sometimes be a long-term suspension, rehabilitation counseling, or both, depending on the school district.

School administrators and criminal justice experts have found the same two factors are effective deterrents for drug involvement and weapons possession: *Punishment must be swift, and it must be certain.* Students must know that if they bring drugs or weapons to school, they will be caught and expelled from school. That message must be loud and clear to all students who attend the school. Adults or off-campus visitors

Figure 7.1   Suggested Body Scanning Procedure

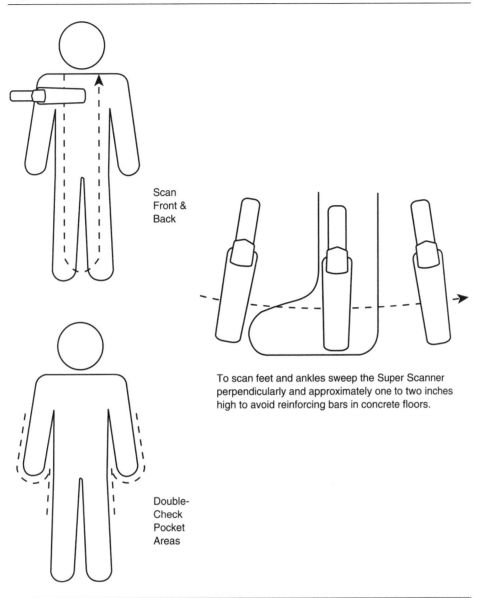

Scan
Front &
Back

To scan feet and ankles sweep the Super Scanner
perpendicularly and approximately one to two inches
high to avoid reinforcing bars in concrete floors.

Double-
Check
Pocket
Areas

who attempt to come onto a school campus to sell drugs or commit acts of
violence will be apprehended and will be prosecuted to the fullest extent
of the law.

A more complete description of what the consequences are for
students discovered with drugs or weapons in their possession is found in
Chapters 3 and 4.

Handling Bomb Threats

Bomb threats are an aspect of weapons prevention that has dogged
schools for many years. Most often they are a hoax, but occasionally a
bomb does explode, and they are a cause of great trepidation and concern
for most school administrators.

Bomb threats create a dilemma. On the one hand, if administrators do not take them seriously, then over a long period of time they run the risk that a device will explode. On the other hand, if an administrator evacuates the school after every call, there may be continued interruption of the instructional process. Not coincidentally, many bomb threats are made around final exam time.

Bomb threats are just what the name implies, threats. Someone who really wanted to blow up the school would probably not give any warning. Bomb threats are usually received by telephone, although there are instances of threats by note or letter. Experienced school administrators and school districts have developed techniques for training secretaries, receptionists, or other school staff who receive telephone calls to listen carefully to a bomb threat and to ask certain key questions. Form 15 is an example of a Bomb Threat Report Form that could be used by a school district to "interview" the caller. A properly completed interview form may be of great assistance to the administrator in charge in deciding whether to take the caller seriously. The school district should have policies in place related to how to deal with bomb threats. This may relieve the administrator of some of the pressure of the decision as to whether or not to evacuate. Some districts evacuate every time a call is received. Others call the police or fire department and have them make a token search and do not evacuate the building. Searching for explosives should be the responsibility of professionals. Most fire departments have someone trained in dealing with explosive devices. There are no magic answers to the dilemma. Once again, it is a judgment call.

CONCLUSION

One of the worst things that can happen to a school is having a reputation as a place where drugs and weapons exist. It frightens students, parents, and the community. It reduces the degree of support for the school. Teachers become discouraged and lose their enthusiasm for their students. Administrators become paranoid and start reacting negatively to every student who is the least bit different. The police department takes a special interest in students from a school with a "bad reputation" for drugs and violence. The principal of the school begins to look for a new assignment.

Schools have found that they can do something about drugs and violence. The types of strategies described in this chapter have been proven to work. Prevention, discovery, remedies, and keeping visitors off school campuses can reduce the incidence of drug abuse and weapons possession in schools. These strategies require a conscious effort rather than great amounts of money. There needs to be a conscious commitment on the part of the entire school staff, the district office, and parents to rid the school of any trace of drugs or weapons. Plans are only as effective as the people who make them.

Form 15   Bomb Threat Report Form

Bomb Threat Report Form

Time and date reported:

How reported:

Exact words of caller:

Questions to ask the caller:

1. What kind of bomb is it?

2. Where is the bomb to explode?

3. When will the bomb explode?

4. Where is the bomb right now?

5. What does it look like?

6. Why did you place the bomb?

7. Where are you calling from?

Description of caller's voice:

Male ____ Female ____ Young ____ Middle-aged ____ Old ____

Tone of voice:
Serious ____ Joking ____ Giggling or laughing ____ Tense ____ Sounded sure ____

Sounded unsure ____ Had an accent ____ If so, what kind?

Is voice familiar? ____ If so, whose?

Were there any background noises?

Other voice characteristics:

Time caller hung up:

Notified:

Name of person answering phone:

Name of school threatened:

Action taken by superintendent in charge:

One of the reasons for the increase in substance abuse among young adolescents is that we have decreased our efforts at drug prevention. During the late 1980s and early 1990s, anti-drug programs were everywhere. The entire nation showed great concern, and, as a result, the statistics went down. No one person is to blame, but the fact of the matter is that as a nation we lost interest in anti-drug programs. Although the public may have lost some interest in drug prevention, school administrators and school boards have not. The number of school districts that still have zero tolerance policies is testimony to the emphasis on anti-drug policies.

Perhaps our concern for drug use was replaced with our fear of the amount of violence occurring on school campuses. New headlines reported a series of violent acts on school campuses. Schools suddenly began to search for ways to "stop the violence." Workshops on the subject of conflict resolution and anger management became popular. Police departments and city governments in large urban areas reacted by expanding the number of officers assigned to schools, and nearly every school in big cities had at least one part-time security officer assigned to its campus. Funds and federal programs suddenly became available.

Despite all the efforts of federal, state, and local programs, drugs and weapons are still omnipresent in our society. Sellers continue to make huge profits despite the tremendous increase in the number of adults being sent to prison. Although there seems to be a decrease in the amount of violence committed by adults, homicides, rapes, and domestic violence still dominate the news. Violence in the media is still a mainstay of plots in fiction. Until society takes serious action against drug and weapons availability in the society at large, schools must continue to educate against the danger of drugs and weapons. It is obvious to most educators that substance abuse is not a fad. The public seems fascinated with violence, and the strategies that schools can use against violence in the media are limited.

Prevention strategies have to play an ongoing role in the curriculum and in school rules, with special programs and with special personnel employed for school safety reasons. We may as well accept that drug and weapons prevention programs are here to stay, and, although the programs may seem redundant for the staff, they are a necessary part of the total school program.

8

School Climate and Its Relation to School Discipline

School climate has been defined as the social and educational atmosphere of a school. A positive school climate helps students feel that they belong and that they are important. A positive school climate is also an atmosphere where parents feel welcomed, respected, trusted, heard, and needed. When parents feel involved, they can help their children succeed in school. Other definitions of school climate emphasize the psychological and institutional attributes that give an organization its personality, particularly group openness and trust (Bulach, Malone, & Castleman, 1994). School climate has been accepted over the years by numerous research studies as a key ingredient of school success and reform. It is also accepted as a key ingredient for a well disciplined and safe school. School climate is the factor that makes a student want to go to school. It is also the factor that makes a teacher want to teach at that particular school. A negative school climate creates an atmosphere that is not good for students or teachers. Administrators have proven to be a key factor in creating positive school climate (Bulach et al., 1994).

THE SCHOOL AS A FRIENDLY PLACE

There is no substitute for friendliness in creating a positive school climate. Some principals may feel it necessary to know each student by name and to stand on the steps and greet students as they come to school. Other administrators like to be present in the faculty room when teachers arrive and to say good morning to each teacher entering the room. Those activities are nice but not really necessary. The important thing is to be friendly throughout the school day to everyone you meet whether it be students, secretaries, parents, campus supervisors, or with whomever you come in contact. This is a difficult thing to fake and is difficult to do when you often have to deal with disagreeable people or situations. Administrators must find their own way to accomplish this sometimes difficult task. Most administrators find humor to be a useful outlet to help keep friendly. Having a few close faculty members or peers to talk to certainly helps. Principals must be careful not to isolate themselves because isolation quickly destroys friendliness. Principals need to pay close attention to their own mental health. Having a family, close friends, hobbies, good health, and a life outside of the school certainly helps.

There are certain personality styles that can destroy a sense of friendliness. Two of the worst offenders are sarcasm and ridicule. Some adults and adolescents who use sarcasm say they were just kidding. Sarcasm is intended to hurt and should never be confused with simple teasing or kidding. Similarly ridicule has no place in the good school administrator's way of dealing with students, teachers, or parents. Humor in the hands of a good administrator is a valuable tool, but sarcasm and ridicule are cheap attempts to find humor at the expense of others. Do not use them.

When school administrators smile a lot they help bring a sense of good feeling to a school campus. Many school situations are not funny and smiling is not always appropriate or easy. When the faculty or students see their administrators smiling, it is a signal that everything is going to be all right. A frown on the other hand may give the opposite signal.

GROUP OPENNESS

Group openness has been described as an interpersonal condition that exists between people in a group when (1) They tell each other what they think about facts, ideas, values, beliefs, feelings and the way they do things, and (2) the willingness to listen to that transmission (Bulach et al., 1994). Group openness is a key ingredient of a friendly school. In a friendly school, there are no forbidden areas, and griping is okay as long as it doesn't go on too long, and it doesn't become a habit. Griping is a basic human right, and if you do not hear it often, it may be sign that people are afraid to say what they really feel. It may be a sign that group openness does not exist.

Faculty members must also have an opportunity to engage in dialogue with other faculty members. For that reason, alternating faculty meetings between large and small groups is important. Some principals have a period by period faculty meeting one month and a full faculty meeting the next. This provides and encourages dialogue. Talking heads at faculty meetings are deadly presentations that should be kept as short as possible. Care must be taken to encourage comments and questions despite the format of any faculty meeting.

EMPHASIZE THE POSITIVE

One of the biggest threats to a positive school climate is an emphasis on what is going wrong rather than what is going well. An example is emphasizing at-risk students rather than the majority of students who are doing just fine. Some negative people like to emphasize the negative because it gives them a sense of importance. It is the school administrator's responsibility to be a public relations person on campus as to what is going right. Administrators need to stay informed as to factual information such as the number of students they expect to go on to college from this graduating class, examples of students who will have good jobs right out of high school, scholarship winners, successful athletic teams, music or drama programs, and so on. They need to publicly praise their best teachers, coaches, music and drama teachers, and so on. They need to know how many students actually have serious discipline problems at school (usually less than 5%) and how many students are truant each day (usually less than 5%). Odds are that the vast majority of students are doing well at the school, but the negative people will use anecdotal information about a few individuals to persuade the listener that all is not well. Good public relations and accurate positive information must become a cause of the school administration.

PROMOTE RESPECT FOR STAFF AND STUDENTS

Respect is something caught and not taught in most schools. Good teachers are generally respected by both students and staff. The mediocre and poor teachers are sometimes the problem. Teachers who do not discipline their students are a problem for building respect for the staff. This is why good teachers need to help poor teachers become better teachers. It is everyone's responsibility, not just the school principal's. It is not unusual for good teachers to give helpful hints to teachers who are having problems. Sometimes principals assign mentors to teachers who are having problems as a way of assisting them in daily tasks and teaching strategies.

The best way to build respect for students by the school administrator is by example. When teachers and staff see the principal treating all students with respect, it is catching. When staff members see the principal listen to students, regardless of how ridiculous the accusation, a baseline is established as to what is acceptable. Conversely when a student or parent demeans someone in public in a disrespectful manner, and those words are confronted by the school administrator, then the administrator is seen as someone who does not accept disrespect. It is one thing to disagree with a grade that a teacher gave and another thing to call the teacher a "fathead" or worse. One is acceptable and the other is not. The tone has to be set that it is possible to disagree with someone without showing disrespect.

PROMOTING CLASSROOM MANAGEMENT SKILLS

The well organized, well disciplined classroom is a major contributor to good school climate. The classroom is the main reason students come to school and classroom management is a primary ingredient to the learning process. A well disciplined class starts on time and is task oriented. Students know what is expected of them when they enter the room. Learning tasks are appropriate and timely. There is no favoritism of genders or groups. There are high expectations, and grading practices are fair. When substitutes are necessary, they are well trained, and teachers have communicated what is expected from the students during their absence. The classroom is orderly and looks like a place where learning is going on. The classroom feels like a good place to be. This includes shop classes, typing rooms, an outside PE area, or a home economics kitchen. There are many types of classrooms, but classroom management skills affect them all.

VALUING DIVERSITY

Diversity is one of the things that has made our nation and our schools great. Fortunately, the kinds of diversity schools have experienced in recent years can only make our schools stronger. There was a time when talking about race, religion, or sexual preference was taboo. In the modern school, openly discussing issues of race, religion, or sexual preference is commonplace. Negative individuals like to use these issues as dividing strategies, but a good administrator recognizes these tactics for what they are: attempts to divide and destroy. Policies, codes, and procedures that attempt to treat students unfairly because of race, ethnicity, religion, or sexual preference must be identified and destroyed, and notice must be made to all members of the school and community that prejudice will not be tolerated at this school. There need to be inservice workshops for teachers and staff about working with diversity at least once per year. Issues change from year to year, and tolerance is too important a topic to ignore. Some staff members need more help than others when it comes to accepting diversity.

SCHOOL CLIMATE AND COMMUNICATION

Good communication is vital to good school climate. As indicated in Chapter 2, a good and updated Student Code of Conduct must be distributed to students and parents annually. The Student Code of Conduct should also be reviewed in the homeroom at the beginning of every school year. Phone calls, letters, progress reports, conferences, personal notes, newsletters, and sometimes small coffee meetings in neighborhoods should be a regular part of communicating with parents and guardians.

Newsletters should be published and distributed at least four times a year. Establishing a speakers' bureau to talk about your school may be an important public relations tool. Appoint teachers and administrators to that speakers' bureau that you know are good speakers. Let service clubs and community groups know about the speakers' bureau. Establish a Web site for your school; posting a monthly calendar of events on it each month may be helpful in communities where parents have computers. Schools must realize when the majority of their parents do not have or use computers. Building administrators must develop public relations skills. Good public relations are an important part of developing good school climate.

SCHOOL CLIMATE AND SCHOOL SAFETY

Although most schools are safe places to be, every effort must be made to ensure that a climate of peace and stability exists. This means that bullying is stopped promptly when it comes to the attention of the school administration, and fights between students are rare. Bullying can be very harmful to the reputation of a school, and every effort must be made to identify bullies and remedies to prevent bullying. Theft is also very harmful to the reputation of a school; methods the school uses to prevent theft should be publicized, and actions taken against thieves should be openly reported. A suspension or expulsion for theft should not be kept confidential. The public must realize that theft is bound to occur whenever any large group of people congregate. Drug sales and use of drugs and alcohol must also be rare, but similarly they should be reported in a manner that keeps them in perspective. Strangers must be kept off the school campus, and supervision of halls, parking lots, and restrooms must be accepted and expected by all. Conflict resolution and anger management skills must be made available to students who need them. Fights and violence should be rare, and consequences swift and expected.

As indicated in Chapter 6, safe schools have safe environments, and safe environments mean fences, lighting, and sometimes locker or book-bag searches. Good students want safety and have accepted what is necessary for a safe environment. Just as citizens have accepted being searched at the airport, students must learn to accept what is necessary to be safe at school.

9

Mental Health and Anger Control as Prevention Strategies

Maintaining the school as a place with good mental health practices has become an increasingly important ingredient for good school discipline practices. Good mental health practices allow the students an opportunity to bond with the positive schooling process despite what they may have learned in a negative home and neighborhood environment. Too often mental health is only considered to be a topic for at-risk students. Good mental health practices should be a part of discipline practices for all students, not just troubled ones. Some of the following mental health practices should be considered by administrators when dealing with students:

1. Identify unnaturally high stress areas for students. Although most normal adolescents can take a large amount of stress, sometimes too much is expected of students by parents, coaches, teachers, or administrators. The current stress on academics for all students may place a large amount of stress on students who do not have verbal or math skills of average ability. The school administrator can play a leadership role in identifying and reducing unnecessary stress in his or her school. The school administrator must help staff understand the difference between healthy competition and irresponsible expectations. Winning at any cost is not a part of the mentally healthy school. Reducing noise levels, having a clean and colorful environment, remaining calm, having a sense of humor, and discouraging

unnecessary competition, sarcasm, profanity, and filth may play a role in stress reduction.

2. Encourage a curriculum that accommodates and meets the needs of all students, not just the academically talented. Unfortunately, the current emphasis on academics and "college for everyone" is limiting the acceptance of those students who do not want or need to go to college. This is a big challenge for today's administrator. Ways must be found to provide learning opportunities and classes for nonacademic students. This means finding a way to keep vocational, home economics, and business curricula. It may mean confronting superintendents, school boards, and parents. This does not mean that principals do not meet the needs of the academically talented, which includes Advanced Placement classes, open attendance at community college classes, distance learning, and humanities programs.

3. Identify depression when you see it. Depression can happen to anyone and frequently does. Knowing that depression is rooted in anger may help a school administrator. We do not expect school administrators to play psychiatrist, but asking depressed students whether they know what they are angry about takes little training.

Signs of depression may include the following:
- A persistent sad or anxious mood
- Feelings of homelessness and pessimism
- Feelings of loss or abandonment
- Feelings of guilt, worthlessness, helplessness
- Loss of interest or pleasure
- Decreased energy, and fatigue
- Thoughts of death or suicide
- Restlessness and irritability
- Persistent physical symptoms
  (Cicchetti & Toth, 1998; National Institute of Mental Health, 2004)

Sometimes, when administrators are dealing with students in trouble, these characteristics are evident, and it may be helpful to know the student is depressed, not insubordinate. Calling a parent and asking about the possibility of the student receiving medical help would be an obvious recommendation. Medications are available that can help students with chronic feelings of depression. Depression is not something that goes away by itself. Students or staff members with depression need help.

4. Identify serious mental illness when you see it. Although unfortunately hyperactivity, attention deficit disorder, autism, and bipolar disorder have become more and more common in our society, identifying the difference is important.

Knowing what a bipolar psychotic disorder means may be helpful when dealing with a student who is way out of the mainstream in terms of student misconduct. School administrators must deal with a lot of complicated disorders in today's world. Once again, school administrators are not psychiatrists, but they need training and continual inservice on mental health issues. It is not only students who could be mentally ill. Sometimes parents may come into the office of the school administrator, and it may become obvious quite soon in the conversation that this person is mentally ill. The school administrator needs to acquire strategies that help to deal with a mentally ill parent. It may be money well spent by the school district to provide inservice training for school administrators on ways to deal with psychotic parents and students. Unfortunately, this has become an increasingly important need (Elias & Branden, 1988).

5. Maintain a list of available mental health services and mental health professionals for parents and have it available as a handout. Many times parents do not know where to turn for help. School district psychologists should be able to help you develop that list. The availability of free resources is especially important in many urban school districts (Power, 2003).

6. Identify when a student is in crisis. Student suicides continue at too high a rate, and sometimes the students who come into the office for a discipline problem are really there because they are asking for help. A skilled administrator knows the difference. Depression can be a sign of a student at risk and should not be taken lightly (Cowen, Hightower, & Pedro-Carroll, 1996).

7. Pay attention to positive school climate. Many of the suggestions in Chapter 8 concerning maintaining a positive school climate apply to maintaining a mentally healthy school. A school that is a happy, positive place where teachers can teach and students can learn is usually a place with a positive mental health atmosphere. The school may be one of the few places in a student's life that does have that atmosphere. Schools can be proud of their role as a good place for young people to learn and grow.

ANGER CONTROL AS A PREVENTION STRATEGY

There is a great deal of anger in our society at present. You only need to turn on the news, look at what is playing at your local theater, or look at the best-sellers list to discover that anger predominates our interest. War, violence, revenge, and punishment are themes for books, movies, television programs, and the news. The school needs to find a way to combat those interests and themes. It is no easy task. Anger management may be a new inservice requirement that schools may need to consider for staff members. Some principles of anger management include the following:

1. Help children determine if their frustration is caused by something they can change. You cannot change who your parents are or your heredity. You can learn to deal with it, however. How you deal with frustration will determine how successful you are.

2. Continually point out the benefits of tolerating frustration. Patience really is a virtue and learning to become patient may help you tolerate frustration.

3. Help children understand that nothing has to go their way just because they want it to. Being a mature person involves learning to deal with frustration.

4. Help children understand that almost nothing is a catastrophe. Helping children and youth understand the old saying "It is not what happens to you that matters as much as how you deal with it" may be helpful.

5. Verbally praise students for their attempts to tolerate frustration. School administrators may be a more important influence in the life of students than they realize. Do not underestimate your praise and its importance.

6. When students do exhibit LFT (low frustration tolerance), point out the consequences of their choices. Another old saying, "There may be reason for your behavior, but there is no excuse for it," may apply (Wilde, 2002).

Deffenbacher (1993) has proposed that angry individuals tend to possess numerous cognitive processing patterns that lead to increased levels of anger.

1. Poor estimation of probabilities—overestimating the probability of negative outcomes and underestimating the likelihood of positive outcomes. Bad things do sometimes happen to good people, but strong people do not become angry at the possibility that something bad might happen. The non-angry individual finds ways to look for the good and sincerely believes that things will turn out alright.

2. Attribution errors—believes negative acts are done intentionally with the express purpose of maliciously attacking one. Anger prone individuals believe they have the ability to read others' minds. It is easy to become paranoid when you are angry because anger sometimes disconnects thinking from reality. The famous "he said, she said" parameters of a fight between two students is a common case in point seen by many school administrators.

3. Overgeneralizations—using overly broad terms when describing time (e.g., excessive use of "always" and "never") and using global descriptions for people (e.g., stupid, lazy, etc.). Unfortunately parents and even teachers are sometimes guilty of overgeneralizations. If they are left uncorrected, they serve as a catalyst for anger.

4. Dichotomous thinking—employing black and white thinking. This type of thinking is irritating to mature people. Helping students

see that things are rarely black and white, and things are usually someplace in between may be helpful in their seeing the truth of situations.

5. Inflammatory labeling—using descriptive terms that are emotionally charged, which only increases the person's anger. This is particularly true in racial issues. Labeling is one of those issues that make people see red. Sometimes people use labels without realizing how inflammatory and hurtful they can be.

6. Demanding-ness—believing others should not act in certain ways, or that they must not behave as they have, in fact, behaved.

7. Catastrophic thinking—evaluating unmet demands in an exaggeratedly negative fashion (e.g., "It's horrible, terrible, and awful that things haven't gone my way"). Things are rarely as bad as we think they are. Asking for someone else's opinion may be helpful in terms of seeing things in their true perspective (Deffenbacher, 1993).

ANGER CONTROL AND HIGH-RISK STUDENTS

Research is helpful to corroborate what many practicing administrators already believe when it comes to noticing how angry some students are and how their anger influences their behavior. Studies have shown that students with high levels of anger have been linked to increased risk for substance abuse, juvenile delinquency, interpersonal difficulties, and vocational and school-related problems (Deffenbacher, Oletting, & Kemper, 1996). Children who manifest high levels of anger at school are also at risk for a number of behavioral, social, and physical concerns and have poorer academic performance. Correlates of anger, hostility, and aggression in children and adolescents are present at school just as they are at home (Smith & Furlong, 1994). Between 21% and 83% of children diagnosed with appositional defiant disorder or conduct disorder were also suffering from a depressive disorder (Angold & Costello, 1993).

There is a real difference between students who misbehave at school because of lack of self control or poor discipline practices at home and students at risk due to great amounts of stored up anger. The school administrator does not have the time or training to truly diffuse the amount of anger present in the at-risk student. The key for the school administrator is to recognize the difference between helping a student who simply needs more structure and helping the student with great amounts of stored up anger. Foster children often have great amounts of anger, and in many cases, it is understandable. Most foster home placement agencies have psychiatric resources available for foster children that can be very helpful. Social workers can also be helpful. Sometimes agencies such as Court Appointed Special Advocates, Big Brothers, and mentors are available. Churches sometimes have groups that help at-risk youth. In any case, the school administrator needs help with at-risk youth.

RELATIONS WITH THE COMMUNITY
AS A PREVENTION STRATEGY

It has become increasingly important for the school administrator to have close contacts with community agencies that deal with youth. This includes law enforcement, social workers, probation officers, county office personnel who deal with truancy, church groups, city recreation departments, and nonprofit community organizations that include at-risk youth or afterschool programs in their mission statements. It might be a good idea for the school administrator to take a lead role in organizing a community youth task force that meets once a month to share programs and needs. Many times resources are available that would be left unused due to lack of information. The task force may also be a resource for funding for grants. Such groups can play an important role in resources for schools, and although they take the time of a busy administrator, they may be worth it in the long run (Epstein, 1994).

Extreme poverty in the community in which the school is located should not be overlooked as an important factor in the success of the school. Research continually demonstrates that schools in areas of poverty have a more difficult time academically as well as socially. Crime and delinquency rates usually go up in economic downtimes and go down in times of prosperity. It is a given principle that the economy influences what happens in communities. Because schools are part of the community, it is inevitable that the economy will influence the school (Jordan, Orozco, & Averett, 2001).

The issue for school administrators is how can they modify the effects of economic downturns in the community upon the school? Unemployment and poverty in a community may undoubtedly play a role in how students see themselves. Unemployed parents or lack of financial resources may cause an effect on student dress or the ability to participate in school activities. Some students may not have the cost of bus fare or gasoline to get to school. Anger and frustration may surface in student behavior because of the effects of poverty.

THE SCHOOL ADMINISTRATOR
AS EMPLOYMENT COUNSELOR

It is difficult to ask the school administrator to play one more role, but the role of employment counselor must be added. The school needs to assign one member of the counseling staff as the contact person for part time jobs available in the community. That person must be aggressive in the search for part time jobs in the area. This is particularly true for schools located in urban areas. That counselor must keep the school administrator in charge of discipline constantly informed of part time jobs available. Those jobs are a valuable resource to the school administrator when dealing with anger and misbehavior that may have its roots in poverty. The reputation of the school administrator as a helping person can be enhanced by practical suggestions and resources that lead to jobs. The community task force can also be an employment resource for the school administrator.

Unfortunately, vocational education is being downgraded in many of our nation's schools. Although Tech Prep and ROP (Regional Occupational Program) programs still exist in most school districts, they often favor students who do well academically in school and look for the already successful student rather than those most in need. There are programs that still exist that can help train needy students for employment after high school. Some of those programs involve contacting local labor unions. Service clubs can also be an important resource because many members have small businesses that may employ recent high school graduates.

CONCLUSION

There is always the possibility that any potential school administrator reading this book would become completely overwhelmed by the task of becoming a school disciplinarian. Being an employment counselor, mental health worker, vocational curriculum advisor, academic analyst, police officer, safety expert, research reviewer, teacher evaluator, community leader, and campus administrator could easily seem to be too much of a job for anyone. There is some truth to that conclusion, but it is also a position that has a great deal of satisfaction. As a school disciplinarian, you have the opportunity to really influence students and make a lifelong difference in what they become. You are also like the mayor of a small town, with all of the political pressure and none of the need to be elected. You can help determine the direction for a school community. You also have the opportunity to develop a philosophy of education that is based on the real world. It does seem that the needs of youth are greater than ever before. Drugs, violence, alcohol, irresponsible parents, and poverty seem to be everywhere, and the school seems to be the one safe place everyone is counting on. Discipline is necessary not because we need to make students conform to some hard nose principles of right and wrong, but because we all need structure in our lives, and school is the place that provides structure for children and youth. Without structure and discipline, human beings become aimless and wander through a life of little meaning and purpose. Structure and discipline make students feel safe and secure. It provides them with an environment that they can count on. In school, students know what is expected of them no matter what they say to the contrary. They want those expectations because it gives them purpose. Good school disciplinarians play a vitally important role in our culture by helping to provide that structure. They teach an unwritten curriculum about fairness, democracy, justice, compromise, caring, and becoming a good citizen. These are lessons that cannot be overemphasized in relation to their importance to our way of life. There is a great deal of satisfaction in knowing that the role you play and time you have spent are truly important and worthwhile. It takes a great deal of energy and dedication, but in the end, it will be worth it.

References

American Medical Association. (1992). Teen violence. *Journal of the American Medical Association, 79*(1), 67–73.

Angold, A., & Costello, E. (1993) Depressive comorbidity in children and adolescents: Empirical, theoretical and methodological issues. *American Journal of Psychiatry, 150*(12), 1779–1791.

Bandura, A. (1973). *Aggression: A social learning analysis.* Englewood Cliffs, NJ: Prentice Hall.

Bertens v. Stewart, 453 So.2d 92 (Fla. App. 2d Dist. 1984).

Bethel School District v. Fraser, 478 U.S. 675 (1986).

Bierlein, C. (1996). *Charter schools: Initial findings, education commission of the states.* Washington, DC: U.S. Department of Education.

Boyle, M. H., & Offord, D. R. (1990). Primary prevention of conduct disorder: Issues and prospects. *Journal of American Academy of Child and Adolescent Psychiatry, 29,* 227.

Bulach, C., Malone, B., & Castleman, C. (1994). *The effect of school climate on student achievement.* Savannah, GA: Georgia Educational Researcher.

Camille Jones, A. (2004, March 7). Kindergarten boy suspended for having a toy knife. *Savannah Herald Tribune,* p. 6.

Cantor, D., Crosse, S., Jhagen, C. A., Mason, K. M., Siler, A. J., & Voln Glatz, A. (2001). *A closer look at drug and violence prevention efforts in American schools: Report on the study of school violence and prevention.* Washington, DC: U.S. Department of Education, Planning, and Evaluating Service.

Cantor, D., & Wright, M. M. (2001). *School crime patterns: A national profile of U.S. public high schools using rates of crime reported to police. Report on the study of school violence and prevention.* Washington, DC: U.S. Department of Education, Planning and Evaluation Service.

Centers for Disease Control and Prevention. (1993). *National survey of high school seniors.* Washington, DC: U.S. Department of Health and Human Services.

Centers for Disease Control and Prevention. (2003). *Illegal drug activity in schools.* Washington, DC: U.S. Department of Health and Human Services.

Cicchetti, D., & Toth, S. L. (1998). The development of depression in children and adolescents. *American Psychologist, 532,* 221–241.

Cleveland Board of Education v. La Fleur, 414 U.S. 632 (1974).

College Entrance Examination Board. (1996). *College-bound seniors: 1995 profile of SAT and Achievement Tests.* New York: Author.

Colorado Revised Statutes, Colo. Rev. Stat. § 22–33–105(4) (1974).

Columbia University Center for Alcohol and Substance Abuse. (1994). *Research study.* New York: Author.

Commonwealth v. Johnson, 309 Mass. 476, 35 N.E.2d 901 (1941).

Cowen, W. L., Hightower, A. D., & Pedro-Carroll, J. L. (1996). *School based prevention for children at-risk: The primary mental health project.* Washington, DC: American Psychological Association.

Crosse, S., Burr, M., Cantor, D., Hagen, C. A., & Hantman, I. (2001). *Wide scope, "questionable quality" drug and violence prevention efforts in American schools. Report on the study of school violence and prevention.* Washington, DC: U.S. Department of Education, Planning and Evaluation Service.

Deffenbacher, J. (1993). General Anger: Characteristics and clinical implications, *Psycologia Conductaul, 1,* 49–67.

Deffenbacher, J., Oletting, E., & Kemper, C. (1996). Anger reduction in early adolescents. *Journal of Counseling Psychology, 43,* 149–157.

Dewey, J. (1913). *Reconstruction in philosophy.* New York: Mentor.

Doe v. Maher, 793 F.2d 1470 (9th Cir. 1986).

Doe v. Petaluma, 830 F. Supp. 1560, 1571 (N.D. Cal. 1993).

Duke, D. L. (1990). School organization, leadership, and student behavior. In O. C. Moles (Ed.), *Student discipline strategies.* Albany: State University of New York Press.

Dwyer, K. I., Osher, D., & Warger, C. (1998). *Early warning, timely response: A guide to safe schools.* Washington, DC: U.S. Department of Education.

Elias, M. J., & Branden, L. R. (1988). Primary prevention of behavioral and emotional problems in school-aged populations. *School Psychology Review, 17,* 581–592.

Epstein, J. L. (1994). *Family and community interactions: A view from the firing lines.* Boulder, CO: Westview Press.

Equal Educational Opportunities Act, 20 U.S.C. 1703 (1974).

Federal Bureau of Investigation. (1995). *Statistical reports.* Washington, DC: Author.

Fein, R., Volssekuil, B., Pollack, W., Borum, R., Modzeleski, W., & Reddy, M. (2002). *Threat assessment in schools: A guide to managing threatening situations and to creating safe school climates.* Washington, DC: U.S. Secret Service and U.S. Department of Education.

Florida State Department of Education. (1993). *Goal five assessment and resource guide* (rev. 4, pp. 93–94). Tallahassee: Author.

Gardner v. Tulia Independent School District, No. 2, WL 3368 02 58 (N.D. Tex. 2000)

Garibaldi, A. M. (1978). *In-school alternatives to suspension: Report to National Institute of Education.* Washington, DC: National Institute of Education.

Gottfredson, G., Gottfredson, D. C., Czeh, E. R., Cantor, D., Crosse, S. B., & Hantman, I. (2000). *National study of delinquency prevention in schools,* Final Report for the National Institute of Justice. Ellicot City, MD: U.S. Department of Justice.

Goss v. Lopez, 419 U.S. 565 (1975).

Grosnicle, D. R., & Sesko, F. (1985). Promoting effective discipline in schools and classroom. *NASSP Journal,* 2(1), 4–8.

Honig v. Doe, 108 S. Ct. 592 (1988).

In re Gault et al., 387 U.S. 1, 87 S. Ct. 1428, 18 L. Ed. 527 (1967).

Institute for Public Policy and Social Research. (2002). Students expelled for bringing inhaler or plastic knife to school. In *Little Tolerance for Zero Tolerance,* Policy Brief, Vol. 4.

Johnson, J. (1996). *Mentoring the future study. Vol. 2: National survey results on drug use.* Washington, DC: U.S. Department of Education.

Johnson, J. (2004, June 23). Public agenda. Teaching interrupted. *Education Week,* p. 39.

Jordan, C., Orozco, E., & Averett, A. (2001). *Emerging issues: Family, and community connections.* Austin, TX: National Center for Family and Community Connections with Schools.

Joy v. Penn-Harris-Madison School Corporation, 212 F.3d 1052 (7th Cir. 2000).

Linke v. Northwestern School Corporation, 734 NE.2d 252 (Ind. Ct. App. 2000).

Males, M. A. (1996, September 18). The truth about crime. *Los Angeles Times,* p. M1.

Michigan State Department of Education. (1992). *Recommendations for a student code of conduct.* Ann Arbor: Author.

Mills v. Board of Education of the District of Columbia, § 615(j) (1972).

Moles, O. C. (Ed.). (1990). *Student discipline strategies.* Albany: State University of New York Press.

Monroe, P. (1918). A brief course in the history of education. London: Macmillan.

Morton v. Ruiz, 415 U.S. 199, 235 (1974).

National Association of Secondary School Principals (NASSP). (1990, January). Procedural due process and fairness in student discipline. *Quarterly Legal Memorandum,* 6–12.

National Center for Education Statistics. (1987). *Public school teacher perspectives on school discipline.* Washington, DC: U.S. Department of Education.

National Center for Education Statistics. (1995). *Drop-out rates report.* Washington, DC: U.S. Department of Education.

National Center for Education Statistics. (1996). *The condition of education, 1996.* Washington, DC: U.S. Department of Education, Office of Educational Research and Improvement.

National Institute of Mental Health. (2004). *Depression: Signs and symptoms of depression.* Retrieved April, 2004, from www.NIMH.com

National School Board Association. (1984). Towards better and safer schools. *American School Board Journal, 152,* 43–48.

New Baunfeis Independent School Dist. v. Armke, 658 S.W.2d 330 (Tex. 10th Dist. 1983).

New Jersey v. T.L.O. 469 U.S. 325 (1985).

No Child Left Behind Act, U.S. Department of Education (2002).

Office of Juvenile Justice and Delinquency Prevention (OJJDP). (1997). *National youth gang survey.* Washington, DC: U.S. Department of Justice.

Power, T. (2003). Promoting children's mental health: Reform through interdisciplinary and community partnerships. *School Psychology Review, 32*(1), 3–16.

Richardson, R., Wilcox, J., & Dunne, J. (1995). Corporal punishment in schools: Initial progress in the Bible Belt. *American Education Research Journal, 32*(2), 616–622.

San Bernardino County Superintendent of Schools. (1995). Overview of expulsion procedures. In *Guidelines on discipline, due process, suspension and expulsion* (p. 23). San Bernardino, CA: San Bernardino County Schools.

School District Guidelines for Expulsion, Wash. Admin. Code § 180–40–275 (1995).

School District Guidelines for Suspension and Expulsion, Cal. Educ. Code §§ 48900, 48915 (1986).

School Rules and Procedures: Requirements, Cal. Educ. Code § 35291.5 (1987).

Short, R. J., & Shapiro, S. K. (1993). Conduct disorders: A framework for understanding and intervention in schools and communities. *School Psychology Review, 22*(3), 362–375.

Smith, D. C., & Furlong, M. (1994). Correlates of anger, hostility, and aggression in children and adolescents. In M. J. Furlong & D. C. Smith (Eds.), *Anger, hostility and aggression: Assessment, prevention and intervention strategies for youth.* New York: Wiley.

Stevens, L. B. (1983). *Suspension and corporal punishment of students in the Cleveland public schools, 1981–82.* Cleveland, OH: Cleveland Public Schools, Office of School Monitoring and Community Relations.

Student Discipline, School Rules, and Procedures, California Education Code, § 35291 (2002).

Theodore v. Delaware Valley School District, 761 A.2d 65 F.2 661 (Penn. Commonwealth Ct. November 20, 2003)

Tinker v. Des Moines Independent Community School District, 393 U.S. 503 (1969).

Title XVI, Fla. Stat. § 230.23(6)(c)(1) (1995).

Todd v. Rush County Schools, 133 F.3d 984 (7th Circ. 1998) Cert denied 525 U.S. 8948 (1998).

Trinidad School District No.1 v. Lopez, Colorado Supreme Ct. (1998).

Trotter, A. (1996, October 23). Zero tolerance policies examined and questioned. *Education Week,* pp. 39–40.

U.S. Department of Commerce. (1994). *Current population surveys.* Washington, DC: Author.

U.S. Department of Education. (1993). *Reaching the goals: Goal six: Safe, disciplined, and drug-free schools.* Washington, DC: Office of Educational Improvement.

U.S. Department of Education. (2000). *School survey on crime and safety.* Washington, DC: National Center for Statistics.

U.S. Department of Education. (2001). *Exemplary and promising safe, disciplined and drug-free schools programs.* Washington, DC: Office of Reform Assistance and Dissemination, Safe, Disciplined and Drug-Free School Programs.

U.S. Department of Education. (2002). *Children ages 12–17 identified as special education students,* Washington, DC: Office of Special Education.

U.S. Department of Education. (2004). *Recent changes in the Individuals with Disabilities Act.* Retrieved June 23, 2004, from Office of Special Education at www.ed.gov/offices/OSERS/OSEP

U.S. Department of Health and Human Services. (1993, June). National health statistics report. Retrieved March 3, 1997, from the *U.S. Department of Health and Human Services Bulletin* Web site.

U.S. Department of Justice. (1995). *Sourcebook of criminal justice statistics.* Washington, DC: Author.

Veronica School District 473 v. Acton, 115 S. Ct. 2386, 2391–92 (1995).

Weber, J. M., & Silvani-Lacey, C. (1983). *Building basic skills: The dropout.* Columbus: Ohio State University, National Center for Research in Vocational Education.

Webster's New World College Dictionary (3rd ed.). (1996). New York: Macmillan.

Wehlage, G. G. (1984). *Dropping out: How much do schools contribute to the problem?* Madison: University of Wisconsin, Wisconsin Center for Education Research.

Wilde, J. (2002). *Anger management in schools: Alternatives to school violence,* 2nd ed. Lanham, MD: Scarecrow Press.

William T. Grant Foundation. (1988). *Work, family, and citizenship: Report on the forgotten half: Noncollege youth in America.* Washington, DC: Author.

Wilson, R. (1995). Phi Delta Kappa/Gallup poll: Parent and public concerns for public education. *Phi Delta Kappan, 20,* 52.

Zerle, P., & Nalvonr, S. (1988). *A digest of Supreme Court decisions affecting education.* Bloomington, IN: Phi Delta Kappan.

Zotti, G. (2004). *Suspension for dad's marijuana.* Retrieved, March 31, 2004, from www.DailyLocal.com

Index

**CORWIN
PRESS**

The Corwin Press logo—a raven striding across an open book—represents the union of courage and learning. Corwin Press is committed to improving education for all learners by publishing books and other professional development resources for those serving the field of K–12 education. By providing practical, hands-on materials, Corwin Press continues to carry out the promise of its motto: **"Helping Educators Do Their Work Better."**